FAKE
IDs

Endorsements

"This book is for anyone who has ever been told they are someone they're not. It is for anyone who has ever felt lost, alone or small. Katie's witty anecdotes provides readers with a feeling that they can relate to her. It shows readers what it looks like to be a woman who has grown to embrace who she is (a child of God). The world tries to tell women we need to be so many different things. This book, on the other hand, challenges you to stop and ask yourself: *What would my life look like if I stopped trying to be perfect, and turned my attention towards the only person who is—JESUS?*

—KELSEY MITCHEN

"As a college girl just trying to figure it all out, *Fake IDs* really transformed how I view myself. With touching stories, helpful ideas, and a bit of humor, Katie Humphress teaches that our value comes from our relationship with God. My identity is based on God alone! A great read for any young woman searching for a few answers."

—MEGAN HOLTHUS, COLLEGE STUDENT

"I haven't read this book, but you should."

– RYLIE (KATIE'S DAUGHTER), FIRST GRADER

"*Fake IDs* is a beautiful book written by a woman who first hand knows what every college girl experiences. I have loved diving over these pages and knowing more about how Jesus loves me even in my messes."

—SARA GAIL FIELDS, COLLEGE STUDENT

"We are all hiding behind something, a Fake Identity replacing who we really are. At the core of *Fake IDs*, the Scriptures offer us truth and a solution to Fake IDs...references to help us find out who we really are."

—LAURA SUE MASON, FORMER MISS KY

"This intimate book embraces any woman who has ever felt defined by her past or present mistakes and changes the way that she understands her real identity. *Fake IDs* paints an honest and vulnerable picture of confusion, exploration, hope and love on every page."

—EMILY CANTERNA, COLLEGE STUDENT

"Working for 30 years with students and women, I have longed for a book that gave women a way out of bad choices. I wish I had this when I was in college!"

—MARIBETH BURTON, FORMER CAMPUS MINISTER

FAKE
IDs

katie humphress

PAVILION BOOKS
PO Box 8653
Lexington, KY 40533

Contact the Author at katie@laneofroses.com.

Printed in the United States of America
ISBN 978-0-9827519-9-2

To Anthony

ACKNOWLEDGEMENTS

Anthony Wallace Humphress: the longer we're married, the more I love you. Thank you for reading this very girly book at least 10,000 times. You taught me that the confusing Christian-y phrase "identity in Christ" really means seeing myself as God sees me. Ten years after confessing that I wanted to write this book, I can because of what you have shown me. Thank you. Thank you. Thank you.

Rylie Jaye, my precious daughter, I thank God every time I think of you. You're so talented, beautiful, kind, and wise beyond your seven years. I love you more than you can possibly imagine. Your joy is contagious; your quotes hilarious. Our coffee dates are so fun.

AJ, you are awesome. I love hanging out with you, and think you have what it takes. I love you and am proud of you. Watching cartoons with you is one of my favorite things to do. So glad you are my son & can't believe you're mine. You're my favorite super-hero.

Mom & Dad: Mom, for seeing potential in me when I didn't see any myself and for teaching me that love can really be unconditional; and Dad for showing me that being a dreamer is a good thing…and for teaching me not to take life so seriously.

Janet, my lovely grandmother, you taught me the importance of having good friends. I love you.

Thank you to my friends who read this whole blasted thing (and gave *tons* of feedback!) when it was twice as long and three times as confusing—Emily Shuter, Holly Shuter, Laura Sue Mason,

Peggy Humphress, Megan Holthus, Maribeth Burton, Cassidy Beymer, Sara Gail Fields, Emily Canterna, Lisa Cooley, Kelsey Mitchen, and Rebekah Clevinger...and again, Anthony. Thank you. Also, Jessica, thanks for being such a good sport & modeling for the cover. Love you.

My mom friends (Amy, Hannah, Sarah, & Megan): I love you so much it hurts. Raising my kids wouldn't be half as fun without you. You keep me sane and keep me moving forward. Your encouragement gives me the guts to do what deep down I know I should be doing.

Lane of Roses girls—wow—I love working with you, knowing you, and sharing www.laneofroses.com with you. Thanks for your vulnerability, encouragement, and strength. I would love to write each and every one of your names down but our little group is growing and I don't want to leave anyone out. Thanks for reading this book, thanks for writing for the site. Texting, emailing, and meeting with you gives me great joy. I hope I can encourage you half as much as you encourage me.

Erika, Melody, and Grace Ann: Thank you for letting light shine through the cracks in your jars of clay. You know what it means to be a Daughter, Friend, and Bride. Thank you for the feedback, thank you for letting me share. And—Elizabeth—you are so very beautiful inside and out. Thanks for letting me share your quotes about your dad. Also, thanks to Emily Canterna the sorority sister who prayed behind the scenes for Grace Ann. No one really ever knew you were praying, but that didn't stop you. I love that.

Thank you to my friend Betty Hoskins for letting us take pictures in your gorgeous home. And Jeff Rogers—both for the pictures and for praying for me at Panera. That prayer changed my life.

Finally, Tommy Green (Publisher, Editor Extraordinaire) thanks so much for playing such a large role in *Fake IDs*. Pavilion Books has made a huge difference in my life. "Writer" was my childhood dream job and now it's coming true. Thank you.

Contents

PART 1

My Dirty Little Secret(s)

Top 10 Things I'd Tell My Younger Self

This book is what I would tell my 20 year old self. It really is. If I could go back in time, I would hand myself this book, tell myself to quit cutting my own hair, and jet back to the future where I happily live with my awesome husband and 2 sweet little kids.

In fact, if I were able to tell my younger self just 10 things—and *only* 10 things—the list would look like this:

1. Someday you will get married and have a family, but—THANK YOU GOD—you dodged a bullet. Your husband is no one you know now.

2. God is not pacing the clouds ready to strike you dead…or at the very least, miserable. Learn about His true character; it will change you.

3. Those friends that intentionally give you bad advice or try to drag you down? They are not your friends. That hurts, but not nearly as much as you will hurt yourself following their bad advice.

4. Eventually you will marry someone you date. Do you really want to marry someone who got fired for stealing from CVS? Think about it.

5. If a hot guy notices you in your tight shirt…so will that old man at McDonald's.

6. Quit beating yourself up. Even about your shirts.

7. Give Christians a fair shot. Some will be obnoxious, but some won't. You need some spiritual guidance right now. Find it.

8. You have many talents, but making your own clothes? Not one of them.

9. College is not the time of your life—and that's okay. Cramming a lifetime's worth of fun into four years is more pressure than it's worth. The best is yet to come.

10. Keep the main thing the main thing. A relationship with Jesus Christ eventually transforms you. It's where you find confidence. You won't have to fake it anymore.

Because of my desire to time travel and tell my younger self what I wish I would have known then, I've spent the last decade of my life mentoring college girls. Even though the sting of my memories is gone, my passion for young women to know their value continues to grow.

I remember how hard it is to "be yourself" when you have no clue who you really are. So if you are in the process of figuring things out too: I know you're searching, trying, working, and striving. I know you're hungry, tired, confused, and lonely. I know you're flipping to the back cover of the book to see if I'm a loser or not. Sure, you're checking me out. But I would have done the same thing at your age…and—okay, okay—maybe I still do.

My hope is that whether you think I'm totally lame/ugly/stupid OR completely awesome/beautiful/smart you at least hear this one thing: *It is what God thinks of you that matters and determines your worth.*

God delights in us in our best moments, but He still loves us in our lowest, most disgusting moments too. As someone with more than a few lackluster moments of her own, this is life-changing news. For this reason, the message of *Fake IDs* is pretty simple:

God loves you. You don't suck.

Even though I grew up in church, I missed this somehow.

The Secret Life and Times of Katie L. Humphress

I'm Katie, mom of the two cutest kids in the whole wide world, and wife of Anthony—the owner of a real estate holdings company in Kentucky. According to Anthony my type is short, bald, and hairy. But that's just part of his charm. He's really funny. And for the record, he looks like Tim McGraw except instead of a cowboy hat he wears a Red Sox cap. Just how I like it.

Besides helping some (an overstatement) with the family business, I've also spent the last decade speaking to college girls about worth and value...which is ironic because when I hear the words "worth and value" I cringe. Value is important, but if anyone walks in a room and says "let me talk to you about your value" it can come across as "let me tell you how awesome I am." That makes me want to throw some punches and roll my eyes. Even if it's me saying it.

Nonetheless, in 2013 I started a website (www.laneofroses. com) as a platform for young women to share stories so others know they are not alone. The website has many free resources on faith, relationships and identity as well. Where you find your value affects everything about your identity…I know because I learned this the hard way.

When I say I did some crazy things in college, I am definitely not bragging; there is a difference between feeling embarrassed, and feeling ashamed. I've experienced both. In fact, if I could go back my main advice would be "Okay, 20-yr-old Katie, think about what you want to do. Got it? Great. Now, do the opposite." I was an idiot.

However, the great news about my deranged choices is that I am in no place to judge. In other words, I get it. I get how hard it is to be young and I never want to forget. Well, I want to forget some things—like the time I farted in Tim Sedlacek's face during sit-ups in 5th grade gym class. But you get my point.

While farting in gym class was not one of my prouder moments, I do have a story that once embarrassed me so much I spent years covering it up. Maybe you can relate. Because if you're like me, your *real* embarrassing situation is one you would never tell because it left you with a broken heart. And at the root of ANY of our problems or risky behaviors is a broken heart…and a whole lot of lies.

Broken hearts and believing lies make us lash out in so many destructive ways. And there are a million ways to get a broken heart, a million opportunities to believe a lie. Maybe we have a broken heart over not being accepted in a group, so we believe a lie that we're not worth accepting and do whatever it takes to fit in. Maybe our childhoods sucked, and we just don't feel worthy of good things. Maybe we're trapped in a downward spiral that started because someone hurt our feelings.

That's my story.

My senior year of high school started off like a dream come true. Believe it or not, I was the cheerleading co-captain and Harvest homecoming queen. I finally had all I ever wanted when I got the news my family was moving 14 hours away. February of my senior year I had to start over at a teeny tiny school. I was crying-on-the-bathroom-floor lonely. By the time summer came around and it was time to start college, I was super vulnerable as well. I felt like a loser, a prime target for a manipulative a-hole.

This part makes my skin crawl: I started dating a guy I wouldn't have touched with a ten foot pole if I had met him one year earlier. Code: Dork Alert. He was a HUGE dork in so many ways, trust me I want to shove him in a locker just thinking about him. But the one thing he did have was the ability to hurt my feelings—to make me believe his lies. He told me I was the nerdy one, and after hearing enough rude comments and feeling so lonely without any of my friends around, I believed him!!! My already insecure feelings were confirmed by that turd of a boyfriend; my heart split in two.

A couple years and (Thank God!) one less boyfriend later, I was in a sorority and became an expert at projecting HAPPY on the outside but aching on the inside. This was especially true for me junior year. It seemed like everything I touched went to crap. The hilarious part is I mean that literally. I took a ceramics class and the pottery I made was hideous—visual proof of my brokenness. All of my pottery was three inches thick on one side and a millimeter on the other. It was messed up, just like me.

Midway through my junior year, I started dating someone halfway decent. Light at the end of the tunnel! I thought the relationship would solve all my problems. A couple times I even took him to my art studio hours—because apparently I was

Boss of the World and could take whoever I wanted wherever I wanted. At any rate, my bliss didn't last long. Two weeks later he dumped me...on the way home from ceramics class...where I made more rotten art.

Freshly dumped, with my new ex-boyfriend trailing 10 feet behind me, I felt lower than low as I schlepped home through campus. That walk home was painful. I can remember every step, every breath. Crushed beyond belief, my spiral got a little worse that semester. A broken heart filled with lies makes you feel like you deserve bad things, and my heart was officially in a million little pieces.

For years I wanted to throw any and all pottery in the trash and forget about it—and believe me I tried. However, I never succeeded because my clueless mom insisted on displaying it throughout our whole house: bathrooms, kitchen, display cases!!! It was everywhere!!! Apparently, the cracks made for excellent flower pots because even the yard was not exempt from my broken-down art.

However, something changed in me and now those ugly pots are in my house too. They are a reminder that God made me, and no matter how broken I am on the outside, His power is in me:

> We now have this light shining in our hearts, but we ourselves are like fragile clay jars containing this great treasure. This makes it clear that our great power is from God, not from ourselves. 2 Corinthians 4:7

I may have parts of me that have broken over the years, but I am NOT a broken person. Sure, I may be a clay pot—but I am a clay pot made by the hands of God! There is no lack of talent in my formation. Inside me is beauty, power, and so much love it can't be contained. God's love burns brightly in my heart.

And light? It shines brightest through the cracks in any vessel. The cracks in my story don't feel like brokenness anymore, they feel like an opportunity to let light shine through. I didn't know that was possible.

Learning that God loves me at my best (and at my worst) changed how I see myself. If God made me the way I am, if He accepts me, and thinks I'm valuable, surely I can accept myself. My value as a person is not dependent on what anyone, myself included, thinks of me. Now, when someone hurts my feelings or I make a mistake, I don't have to punish myself or hit the self-destruct button. Instead, I remember I have a treasure in me; I'm valuable.

However powerful any realization, change doesn't happen overnight. For years after I graduated I would be going about my day and suddenly a song or smell would trigger an unpleasant college memory. As you read that sentence, I'm sure images of your own immediately flashed through your mind too! However (and I did this with a Christian counselor) I eventually confronted those memories and was very surprised at the result.

The counselor asked me to picture my worst memory, what it smelled like, what it looked like, what I was wearing—or not wearing—and imagine where God fits in that picture. To my surprise, when I pictured God in the room of my worst college memory, He was not shaking His head with a grimace on His face. Instead, He looked at me with compassion and invited me into a hug. Is that crazy?

I don't think so.

The image of a compassionate God inspired me to read the Bible for more clues about how God really feels about me. When I did, it changed my life. Turns out, God loves me more than I bargained for:

And may you have the power to understand, as all God's people should, how wide, how long, how high, and how deep his love is. May you experience the love of Christ, though it is too great to understand fully. Ephesians 3:18-19a

A broken heart tricked me into believing a lie that I was worthless. I felt dirty, so I lived dirty. Feeling worthless is a risk you don't have to take. When my behavior felt out of control and I couldn't make it stop, I was really just harboring wound after wound. Once I addressed my heart with the truth, I began to heal and my behavior sort of changed automatically. It's not like I tried to change, it just happened as a result of finally believing the truth.

Any heart can heal. You. Are. Valuable. You are worth it. You can change. After all, God is the potter, we are the clay. And God is in the business of creating masterpieces, not crap:

For we are God's masterpiece. He has created us anew in Christ Jesus, so we can do the good things he planned for us long ago. Ephesians 2:10

But That's Not All...

Clearly to me the worst feeling in the world is believing a lie about yourself. I believed I was damaged goods, broken, helpless, out of control—and it sucked. And while I don't think a broken heart is ever funny...I did have one habit in particular that was so bad it was ridiculous. And if I'm not careful, I find myself repeating this old habit (comparing myself to others) again and again.

But let's talk about someone else's dumb mistake first. A few years ago during sorority recruitment one member made a list—an actual written down on a piece of paper list—of all the girls in her house and how she perceived them. She divided the girls into categories like "Rich" "Put up Front at Recruitment" and "Needs a Makeover." It caused quite the stir when a disgruntled list member found it and distributed copies to all the other sisters. Drama.

Of course, my response to that story was shock: "How cruel! And *what a dummy.* Who puts that stuff in writing anyway?!?!" And then I remembered something.

I had a list system too.

When I relied on my own merit to get ahead I had mental lists (I hope I never wrote anything down, but who knows) of anyone and everyone who was better/worse than me. I would love to say that I started this list system as a vulnerable twenty-year-old and it's really a mean boyfriend's fault, *bbbuuuuuttttttt...*it started much earlier than that.

As a chubby kid (who apparently farted a lot), I felt like I was always on the bottom of every list I cared about: cool, popular, beautiful. I was the lowest ranked in every category. I still remember the name of cutest girl in 2nd grade. It wasn't me.

When I finally scraped my way up the ladder to become head cheerleader, student body officer, and homecoming queen the view was breathtaking. Take that, suckers! Try not picking me for the kickball team now! But my joy lasted about one whole day. Then, I became obsessed with maintaining my spot at the top and the harder I tried, the farther I slipped back down my imaginary ladder. To compensate for my shortcomings on one list, I would work harder to gain better footing on another list.

I was the get-voted-for-stuff type of popular, not the wild party type. My brother actually said I was just better at getting the dork vote. To feel better about myself—and because I had no serious boyfriend and my closest friends didn't drink—I found value in my unbelievable self-control and judged anyone who drank or slept around. Juggling all those lists was a nightmare. And every single list was rooted in a big fat lie that my spotless performance, looks, and affirmation from others gave me validation.

With a head full of lies, it took about two seconds to get knocked off my horse when I started college. After my drinking and boyfriend behavior flew out the window, I fell about halfway down the list compared to others I knew at the time. That made me feel bad, so I compensated by trying harder at something else. I would fail at that, fall down a little more, and compensate elsewhere. That was the cycle: claw my way up a list, fall down, claw my way up, fall down, claw my way up. Repeat.

No matter how hard I pushed myself to become a better person, I always came up short. Hitting rock bottom on a list is hard because there is always a new low. A new list. If I came up short on a list, it was easy to make a new one. The problem with creating a list of people better or worse is there will always be a higher high than you can reach, and there is always, most definitely a lower low. You don't have to test this out. Just trust me.

I joined a sorority junior year because I had exhausted my other lists of people and needed a new group so I could start over. Maybe get the fresh start I craved. Overall, my sorority could have been the perfect place to develop some meaningful friendships. However, I used the opportunity to create yet another brand new list system.

Contrary to my mom's frugal ways, I somehow found out we were not actually poor so I added "rich" to my list of good qualities. My roommate in the sorority house was also "rich" (in quotes so I don't puke) and we bonded quickly because I found out she had lists too. According to our made up system we were both doing really well compared to our other sisters:

☑ Rich, check!

☑ Pretty, check!

(ummm…I was obviously in denial. Apparently when I feel bad about myself on the inside, it shows on the outside. Here's a snapshot: dark circles, beer gut, and self-inflicted haircut.)

☑ Boyfriend, check!

(wow, denial again…what was I thinking?!)

Anyway, my roommate and I were both insecure wrecks. We eventually turned on each other to the point we would pass on campus without making eye contact—classy, right? And like Tracy Jordan jokes on *30 Rock*, people who say they are classy usually are.

My point in telling you all this is that I never got anywhere on my own. I just traded one list for another until I felt like giving up. And I did. I would create new lows, new lists, new friends. Like a hamster on one of those little exercise wheels, I just kept on spinning (maybe that's why I hate spinning classes so much).

If you want to keep doing what you're doing to try to be "happy" on your own—knock yourself out. I've been there, and as an Overachieving Overachiever I promise that choosing to believe lies (I can be better if I do X, Y, or Z) will only make you more miserable, empty, and less fulfilled. It's a bleak picture.

You were made for more than a constant cycle of never measuring up and believing lie after lie after lie. Lies force you to create a phony image of yourself. And there is *nothing* more depressing than pretending to be somebody you're not.

However, I eventually switched directions. Now I don't believe I suck compared to others…because I know I suck completely and totally on my own! The great news is I'm okay with that because God loves me anyway and *through Him* I am perfect. Through my faith in Jesus, I can chuck any and all lists out the window because it's what God thinks of me that defines me and determines my worth.

In college, I would scrape my way up a list only to wind up feeling dirty and ugly compared to someone else. Putting my faith in God changed all of that. My external looks, the amount of money in my bank account, the number of friends I have, none of it makes me any more or less valuable. I'm valuable because God thinks so, and I have to tell you, one side effect of *believing* I'm valuable is *living* like I am valuable.

When I was consumed with my lists, I always felt worse and more and more out-of-control in the end. Now, the more I get to know Jesus (by spending time praying and reading His Word) the more I realize He died so I have access to HIS security, HIS peace. I'm no longer out-of-control. Not because I'm trying harder, but because I know I'm loved and Jesus is living in me and through me.

Even though I hated certain moments of being "young and free" (I for one felt anything but!) I certainly learned a thing or two. Mostly the hard way, but broken-hearted and full of list after list of how I would never measure up I finally saw the light. I'm learning what it means to be myself, and even better, I don't have to fake it anymore.

PART 2

FAKE IDs

— Fake IDs —

What is a Fake ID?

Seeing Yourself as Others Perceive You

Eek. I had a Fake ID once. It's especially embarrassing because I got it two weeks before my 21st birthday, but I had one nonetheless. After my parents and I moved my senior year of high school, I went back to visit my group of best friends several times throughout college. On one visit my friends suggested we go to the hot new bar in town. Anyone who was anyone would be there—we had to go.

Now, it's only fair to say the "hot new bar" was actually a family-style restaurant by day and a "club" at night but it was the place to be. The only problem was it was 21 and over. Since I was the oldest in my group I wondered how they had gotten in since none of us were old enough. It turns out my best friend's older brother had made them all Fake IDs in her basement. Problem solved! My joy was short-lived however because the IDs were terrible.

And by terrible—I mean one was on the back of a Taco Bell gift card—terrible...and that was the good one. Another was on the back of a novelty "fart card" somebody had gotten as a joke. In the end, since he was fresh out of fart cards, her brother ended up using rubber cement to glue new dates on my actual driver's license. It was the worst. We got in the club, but it was clear any old ID, no matter how fake, would get you through the door. At least mine didn't have a "smell-o-meter" on the back.

I remember thinking that night was sure to be spectacular. And in terms of fun it was alright. I saw a popular guy from high school and—gasp—he almost said hi. He was either nodding to me or someone directly behind me, but I didn't care. At the time, it was close enough and I felt awesome about it. But eventually cheap thrills and almost-encounters weren't enough. I wanted more.

And eventually, I found more. Really the timing of meeting my husband and trusting God for everything happened eerily at the same time. I say eerily because for a while I was worried my husband was just one more boy I was trying to impress, trying to get to notice me. Anthony was working in campus ministry at the time, and when we got married I decided to join him. Despite a lingering fear I was out to impress Anthony with my newfound holiness, I was excited about it.

Not surprisingly, the title "campus minister" was a whole lot of pressure for someone starting over like me. In fact, I felt like I was still in my friend's basement furiously slapping rubber cement on a Fake ID. Except instead of pretending to be 21 I now felt like I had to pretend to be an extremely wise and mature Christian who enjoyed quietly reading her Bible for nine hours a day.

However, I couldn't fake "extremely wise and mature" for very long. Which makes me laugh because what's coming next is sure-fire proof: At my first ever nation-wide retreat for campus ministers, I dropped an F-bomb...*in front of everybody.* And I didn't just drop it. I threw down my pencil and *SCREAMED* it in front of a group of 100 or so other ministers.

But they deserved it and here's why: To make the retreat more engaging, someone had the bright idea to have a Soduku challenge. For other non-mathy people like me, a Sudoku puzzle is some sort of math strategy, numbers, patterns sort of game. I'm still not completely sure.

Anyway, one person from each randomly assigned team had to complete a Sudoku puzzle, and the first to finish won a point for their team. My team pushed me to the crowded game table as I stammered, "I don't know what this is! Not me! Please! Not me!" and the whistle blew. When one nice teammate tried to help me, everyone else in the circle yelled "No cheating!" That shot through me like a bolt of lightning. Cheating? I didn't even know what Sudoku was!! I stood up, threw down my pencil, and yelled "F@#* it!" as I stomped out of the room and slammed the door.

See? Told you they deserved it.

At any rate, this story represents the early stage in my journey to find an Authentic Identity. When I met my husband 10 years ago, he asked me what I wanted to do with my life. I said, "write books on self-esteem for college girls" without having a clue what that really meant. You see, Anthony and I met my first year out of college and attended this conference exactly one year later...which means I was fresh off a series of horrendous choices and experiences.

I was so grateful for Anthony—especially for being interested in a messed-up person like me—and I threw myself in campus ministry (something I had previously despised) to prove how changed I really was. I thought "self-esteem" was what I needed in those low times and it took me several years to understand that self-esteem won't get me anywhere without Jesus Christ. Self-esteem on its own just gets me frustration and f-bombs in the end. It seems like a good thing, but there is no freedom. I believed in God, but still depended on myself.

Turns out, good self-esteem can be just a professional grade Fake ID. After all, self-esteem really is less about esteem and more about effort in the end. And there's a difference between self-effort and surrender. You can keep relying on your own effort to make yourself happy, or you can give your cares, anxiety, and life to God. **Relying on God versus relying on yourself is the difference between an Authentic ID and a Fake one.**

As for me, it's very clear. I need help. I need God or I'm just a hothead with a potty mouth. On my own I focus on the 10 zillion horrible scenarios that are going on in the world and ignore the good. It's why I don't watch the news. I get my current events from cartoons on Netflix. Even if I manage not to hear anything awful, terrible images still flash through my mind when I lay down at night.

Now, if I am really such a nervous wreck, how do I ever get any sleep? I remember that I am not in control. I remember that God will make everything right. I remember that just as many wonderful things happen at the same time as all of the terrible things. Then, I read some cookbooks (hey, there's no harm in distraction) and fall asleep; I surrender.

No matter what I say, or how hard I try to persuade you to choose what I think is right, the choice is still yours: trust God or trust yourself. Because I'm older, I can tell you what my life was like, and what it is like occasionally, when I decide to do things on my own terms. I can tell you what happens when I swap my Authentic Identity (what God thinks of me) for a Fake one (the lies I think, or others think, about me).

Growing up, I knew I had it made, and felt guilty that my ideal circumstances didn't make me happy. I always wanted something better, something more. But my problem was that the harder I tried to be happy, the less I actually was. I remember driving around in my dad's jeep when I was in high school, bummed because even though I finally had everything I ever wanted, it wasn't enough. That's me. Never satisfied. And knowing I was a brat who was never satisfied didn't help either. However, a flip switched in my thinking and in my heart and I learned a better way.

Negative self-talk, ugly memories, lies, and circumstances beyond our control all contribute to how you see yourself. I once knew a girl who swore the whole school (school as in *university*) talked about her because of how she acted with guys. When she decided to follow God she was grateful He accepted her past and all. I was thrilled she recognized God loves her, but I also had to smile because there is no way everyone was talking about her. People are too busy obsessing about themselves to worry much about anyone else.

Even as I listened to the girl pour her heart out, I noticed some people I knew at the restaurant and wondered how my hair looked that day. It's just how it goes. Sure, I cared about the girl and her problems, but I couldn't help but wonder about myself too. People are selfish: *Hmmm, your story is great and all but where do I come in?*

You will always think your story is better/worse compared to someone else because it's hard not to make yourself the hero/villain of your story. It makes sense. You are the main character in your own life, but you aren't the *only* character. Besides, comparing ourselves to others never gets us anywhere. There is always someone more outrageously bad and there is always someone more outrageously good. Virgin or sexpot, we all think our stories are the most embarrassing, the hardest to overcome.

However, God doesn't see you based on how you see yourself or how others perceive you. He sees you as His Creation, His precious Daughter. And no matter where you've been, He wants you to come home.

So after years of sitting across from girls in coffee shops and hearing "I know I'm the only one" approximately 1,543,998 times, I thought—wow—it's a shame I can't connect all these girls somehow. If they only knew how very *not* alone they all are, surely that would give them some hope.

That's why www.laneofroses.com was born. Lane of Roses is a collection of experiences. It's my experience and the experience of the many girls who share their stories on the website. Sharing stories breaks down the lie that everyone else is perfect, and we are the only ones who don't have it all together. We can be weak because showing weakness is ultimately what makes us strong. When we get to a place of vulnerability, it's not about us anymore—and that's when miracles happen.

In some ways it's fun to look back at my own life and slap my hand to my forehead about all the many ways I tried to define myself. My parents recently downsized and my mom gave me a box loaded with old pictures of myself from birth till post-college. Man, my hair has been every possible length, and thanks to an unfortunate hair dye accident, nearly every color. I've gained weight; I've lost weight. I've dressed like a nun; I've dressed like a—well—opposite of a nun. I laughed and I cried over some of those pictures, but the one thing I'm grateful for the most is that now, even if my hair changes or my weight fluctuates, my identity stays the same. Because I put my faith in God, I am His; I'm His child, His Friend, His beloved Creation.

Fifteen years post identity crisis I can promise you one thing: there is always someone who can relate to your past. No experience, background, or choice is unique. You are, but the individual events in your life are not. Whether your parents cared too much or not enough, whether you feel less than or better than, you are not the only person to feel the way you feel. Don't limit yourself because of your past. Your future is a blank page, a fresh start. You don't have to hide from the past and pretend to be okay; you can be okay.

When I tried to find satisfaction in relationships, looks, popularity, and performance it was all in vain. Even when I snagged a boyfriend, won the vote, or dressed right and achieved a fitness goal I still felt empty and fake. Reaching the top of the list was never enough.

It was like I had a few sets of Fake IDs with the following themes: Life of the Party, Perfectionist, and Girlfriend. Because I couldn't figure out who I was, I would scrape through life swapping one Fake ID for another. If I wasn't invited to a house party, I would date some guy, and when that all failed I would put more pressure on myself to be perfect. Sometimes I would try a combination of identities.

Nothing ever satisfied because none of the Fake IDs were ever really me and it took too much effort to maintain any of those images for any length of time. In the end, all of those ways of defining myself were dead ends…and not a whole lot better than the ID my friend made on the back of a fart card.

If you are sick of defining yourself based on your relationship status, popularity, looks, and smarts—you're not the only one. I've been there, and so have many others, including three girls who agreed to share their stories (that were originally posted on Lane of Roses) as well. All three girls used the same Fake IDs that I did at one point. IDs based on fun, performance, and relationships. Eventually they came to the conclusion that maybe, just maybe, they were made for more too.

Grace Ann, Melody, and Erika: You are proof we are not alone. Thank you.

Fake ID #1

Grace Ann: The Life of the Party

Grace Ann's story is unique because I prayed for her for a year without ever knowing her. One of her sorority sisters came to my house every Tuesday for a Bible study and her prayer request every time was for Grace Ann, one of the most popular girls in their house...and by popular, in this case, I mean wild.

Fast forward a year and this adorable, soft-spoken girl showed up at my house for Bible study, sweet as pie, and I instantly loved her. She said her name was Grace Ann and I really didn't think much about who she really was...until one day she was telling the group a little about herself and it hit me. This was the girl I prayed for all last year!! I just about fell out of my chair!!! Grace Ann and I got to know each other pretty well that semester, as our stories are pretty similar. Here is her story in her own words:

God was always chasing after my heart, but I spent most of my life running from Him...especially during my first two years of college. When junior year finally rolled around I had run so far from Him that I thought there was no turning back, and sadly I was okay with that. I didn't care about a relationship with God because I didn't know what it was like to have one.

I sank into a life of intense partying. I made terrible decisions that seemed fulfilling at the time, yet they ultimately left me numb. I was constantly surrounded by people, but I felt alone and empty. None of my decisions seemed wrong at the time, but eventually the shame caught up with me and I felt worthless.

What gets me about Grace Ann's story is not what crazy things she may or may not have done, but that she felt worthless and alone. I can certainly relate to being in a crowd of laughing people, and even laughing myself, but feeling the exact same way. When I attempted to get my kicks through partying, I felt shortchanged—but I sure didn't act like it.

In fact, a few months ago I was at a restaurant near campus with my little boy and a group of sorority girls came and sat next to us. They were all loud, but there was one girl in particular that had to out-do, out-loud, and one-up all her friends. She was totally obnoxious. And *could not* take a hint. Every mother (okay, okay—it was me!) in the sub shop shot her dirty looks for her graphic play-by-play of what she did last night. When one of the other girls chimed in with a sensational story of her own, she topped it. It was unreal.

Something didn't sit right with me about the restaurant experience. It made me sick. To me, no one is more precious than Grace Ann. But those girls? They were mean, gross, loud, and proud of it. And then it hit me. They may have acted mean, gross, and loud—but the pride thing? Sure, maybe it's fun to shock a group of your friends with your own brand of outrageousness, but eventually you will have to be alone and quiet with your thoughts. Either in your room, walking to class, taking a test, driving to work, eventually all of those girls would be alone. Then how would they feel? I felt like a hypocrite for being so judgmental. When I was in their shoes the nights were sometimes fun, but the mornings were not so great.

My own voice is super loud, so if that had been me sitting with a group of girls 12 years ago, I may have been the most obnoxious one too. Not on purpose, but because loud is my nature and I was so consumed with myself and trying to be happy, that I rarely noticed anyone else either. They weren't trying to destroy my three-year-old's innocence. They just plain didn't notice anyone but themselves. That's what happens when you're secretly miserable. You get so consumed with your own happiness—getting it, keeping it, making others think you have it—all you think about is yourself.

My frustration melted into compassion towards them (which would totally piss them off if they knew it!) and I remembered why I'm so passionate about telling girls they are valuable and loved. No matter how loud or how outrageous the story, each girl has to eventually be alone. Having been there myself, I know all she really wants is to be okay.

So, if you're like Grace Ann, myself, or the restaurant girls you can see why being labeled as "The Life of the Party" is no Authentic Identity at all. **Sure, you may be boisterous and The Life of the Party in public, but when the confetti settles, can you settle?** Can you be alone with your thoughts and, I don't know, like yourself? Like your life? The guy you hooked up with when you were super drunk, the things you said when you were completely high, are you okay with that?

You're not okay because you have feelings. You *can* be embarrassed. You don't have to play the fool forever. You don't have to walk to class the next day praying someone from the night before doesn't recognize you. If you want, you can change. You can trade your empty, embarrassing, exhausting party self for one that truly has a good time.

But with that being said, the first thing I thought when Christians claimed to be hap-hap-happy when I was in college was "Oh, brother. What kind of lame-o event are they calling a good time?" So, for the record: I still think root beer kegs are lame too.

Although I may not enjoy a baby pool filled with jello either (we actually had to change the carpet in an entire rental house after a jello party. Thanks a lot. We *so* appreciate it.) I know a good time when I see one. Now that my identity is based on something more than my weekend plans, I have more fun than ever...and the best news is that I still like myself the next morning.

I couldn't say that before.

Drinking, Drugs, and Dog Turds

If you are stuck in a cycle of constant partying, odds are you've gone too far at least a time or two. Partying is fun until things get a little out of hand and before you know it you've gone farther than you ever intended. Suddenly you're trapped in a pattern that feels impossible to break: shameful memories cause more shameful behavior which cause more shameful memories...but it doesn't have to stay that way.

The first time I ever smelled pot, I thought it was a dog turd. I'm not kidding. I was sitting in a guy's apartment with a bunch of people and shouted, "Ew, gross! *What* is that smell?!!?! There's a dog turd in here! Why would you let a dog poop in your hallway?!?!" Well, I sure felt dumb when the girl next to me informed me otherwise.

I also remember the first time I came across a group of people doing cocaine. It was in a fraternity basement where I'd hung out several times before. I felt so naive. I'd seen all these people a hundred times before and never knew they did "actual" drugs. Even at my wildest, I have to admit that's one thing I never did—I tell you this not to make you feel bad if drugs are a part of your story, but because it's the truth. My mom told us that if you smoked pot your children would have chicken wings instead of arms. I plan on telling my kids the same thing because it worked on me; I never did drugs. However, this group of people knew that about me and it was almost like they were using behind my back. I was hurt and embarrassed...but thank goodness not so hurt I joined the club.

So I'm going to stick with what I know, and I'm going to focus on drinking because if you are over 21 it is legal. If you have a problem with drugs—like I said cocaine was huge at Ohio State when I was there—you need some professional help. Drugs are not legal, and the consequences for getting caught and becoming addicted are huge. Huge. A lifetime of secrecy and one new low after another is not pleasant. Get yourself to a counselor pronto before it's too late. I'm serious. Stop reading and call right now. I've listed several on www.laneofroses.com. While you're at it, read the article about replacing bad friends with good ones. I'll wait.

Great. Now, again, my intention is not to make you feel like crap if you have a drug problem and encourage you to drink instead. I sometimes wonder if alcohol doesn't do more damage than certain drugs. However, I am NOT encouraging anyone to drink who is underage or has alcoholic tendencies...or any other health concerns for that matter. I hate to even write about drinking because it stirs up so many extreme opinions.

Some Christians think drinking is a sin, some don't. Some call it a "grey area" and others say it's black and white. However, I love you and I know you want specific advice. If I've been asked once, I've been asked a thousand times what I think about drinking. So here goes:

1. Know your limits.

Drinking and drunk are two different things. From what I have read in the Bible it is okay to drink, not okay to get drunk:

> *Do not get drunk on wine, which leads to debauchery. Instead, be filled with the Spirit, Ephesians 5:18 NIV*

Now, I'm no math whiz by any stretch of the imagination, but a big gulp from a gas station is always bigger than a Dixie cup. Got that? Big Gulp > Dixie Cup. One time I was dumbfounded when I got skunk drunk after just one beer…until it hit me. A big gulp is *not* just one beer. Duh.

Pay attention to the size of the glass you are using at any party or event. For a better idea of what a serving of alcohol looks like, consider a measuring cup is 8 fluid ounces. That's tiny!!! And a mixed drink is never a good idea because a bathtub full of Bahama Mama's is not measured out with responsible drinking in mind. If you can't tell how much alcohol is in something— hello—that's a red flag. Don't go there. Handling your liquor is not the issue. If you are a woman, you just can't drink as much as a guy (and of course there are exceptions) because your muscle mass is different.

Gosh. I hate being so serious, but over the years I've noticed a shocking truth: sexual assault is way more common that you'd think. I mention this in the drinking section because it happens a lot when alcohol is involved.

Listen closely: I'm *not* saying if you drink a beer, you will get raped; but I *am* saying that drinking too much, from a cup you didn't pour yourself, or from a cup that has been out of your sight for a minute or two puts you at a bigger risk for date rape and other tragedies. It seems like it's easier for a guy to take advantage of a girl who is not fully in control of her faculties— and it's harder to fend off a guy who is not fully in control of his.

Date rape is sometimes a fuzzy line. Waking up in a stranger's, or sadly even a friend's, room with no memory of what happened is scary. Sometimes rape is brutal and direct, but sometimes girls are left with a whole lot of unanswered questions. They don't really know what happened, but they are still in a lot of pain.

Whether or not you can recall the details, you will want the memory or the confusion to go away. And it won't unless you deal with it. If this is you, please go process this with a counselor. Like, now—not tomorrow—now. Way too many girls suffer in silence and it's unnecessary. Unfortunately, you are not the only one. You can heal; you can move on. Start today. See www.laneofroses.com for details on reputable counselors.

2. Respect others.

Also, if your drinking puts someone in an awkward position, be considerate of her feelings. Just because you have the right to drink doesn't mean you should:

> Be careful, however, that the exercise of your rights does not become a stumbling block to the weak. 1 Corinthians 8:9 NIV

A while ago, I heard of a very popular sorority president everyone assumed drank like a fish because she was so fun and social. My friend ran into her at the drink table at a party, and was shocked when the president filled her cup with Diet Coke. She was a respected, fun girl and no one realized (or cared) that she was drinking Coke most of the time. If you choose to abstain, you can still socialize.

3. Think for yourself.

Don't let peer pressure make your decisions for you:

> Walk with the wise and become wise; associate with fools and get in trouble. Proverbs 13:20

The assumption is that peer pressure stops out of high school, but that's not true. There might be more in college—or even post-college where there's the idea of keeping up with the Joneses too. Regardless, it's important to think for yourself no matter what stage of life you are in because living up to an image that you don't really like? It can destroy you.

As a general rule I hate sports, but there was one player at OSU that everyone in our football-crazed state called *The Beast*. He was so famous that even I knew about him. Fans kissed his butt and showered him with attention...until he made some cocky comments in a magazine and everyone turned on him.

In an interview he admitted that to reclaim his fame, he thought he had to live up to the image his admirers expected. Prove he really was worth admiring. Become The Beast. And it didn't take long—he spent much of the next decade in prison for some pretty brutal behavior. However, after years of searching he is seeking God. Turns out, he is not the monster everyone thought. He writes poetry and gives motivational talks to inner-city kids. He's finally thinking for himself.

If you are "The Beast" of partying in your immediate sphere of influence, or you want to be, don't believe the lie that you are nothing more. In fact, if you passed out drunk in the middle of a pool table with a lamp shade on your head last weekend, don't fret. The embarrassment will fade, my friend, it will fade. A lot of times we pretend to laugh off some of the embarrassing things we've done—or get raging mad if someone suggests we have a problem—but don't let the opinions of others drive your behavior. You don't have to live up to your reputation if you don't like your reputation. Sometimes defensiveness is a clue you're on the verge of needing a lifestyle adjustment.

You are allowed to change. Reach out for help if you need it. There's no shame in wanting something different for yourself. Depending on God for courage and contentment is satisfying; it's okay to explore that.

I hope this helps iron out some questions you may have about drinking. I'm not in to telling people what to do, but in this case I feel like I have to add: Please don't break the law and never, ever, *ever* drink and drive!!!!!!!! DUI's are extremely common. If you have one, please don't feel so guilty you spiral out of control. Take it as a wakeup call, be honest with some people who care, and take it as an opportunity to make some exciting changes in your life. Wake up calls can be just what it takes to shake you up and set you on a different course.

Partying to Forget

I can hear the collective roar of nervous stomachs from here to Ohio as I prepare to unload embarrassing family secrets. Kidding!! I am no dummy. I would never, ever write about my own family because A.) they know where I live; and B.) I love them too much. At any rate, I think everyone can agree family dynamics can be a source of occasional stress and frustration regardless of the amount of drama involved.

No matter what our family history, too sheltered or not sheltered enough, our backgrounds can cause us to go off the deep end for a couple reasons. For some of us, we are just trying to forget the pain of the past instead of forgiving the ones who hurt us. For others, there's the concept of FOMO, or the fear of missing out.

I thought about asking a few people to write about their experiences with partying as a way to forget the past. However, getting several family members on the same page is not easy. That leaves me writing about Joseph because he has been dead for thousands of years. No one can get pissed!!!

Joseph's story is one of my absolute favorites. His dad had two wives, one he was tricked into marrying and never loved, and one who was the love of his life. The love of his life had two sons, Joseph and Benjamin. Joseph's mother died after having Benjamin and their father loved them more than his ten other sons, especially Joseph.

Even though Joseph was not the oldest of the twelve sons, his father treated him as such and played favorites big-time. He even bought Joseph a special "coat of many colors" (might ring a bell if you love Broadway plays) that signified that he would be treated as the firstborn which was very important in their culture.

Anyway, Joseph's brothers despised him and planned to kill him. One of the brothers convinced the others not to kill him, so they compromised. The brothers sold him as a slave to some traveling Egyptians. After some major ups and downs as a slave in Egypt, which included jail time after a false accusation from a rejected woman, Joseph eventually rose to second in command of the entire country during a famine he predicted after interpreting the Pharaoh's dream. During the famine, Joseph's brothers (the ones who sold him into slavery!) came to barter for food.

After a dramatic scene that left the brothers terrified, Joseph said:

You intended to harm me, but God intended it for good to accomplish what is now being done, the saving of many lives. Genesis 50:20 NIV

Joseph forgave the brothers who sold him into slavery!! He had every excuse to party like a rock star and blame his family for his problems…especially because his family directly caused his problems!! However, he chose to see his life as a story with twists and turns, many of which were unpleasant, that led him to a greater purpose.

Your family is not perfect. My family is not perfect (oops, I've said too much). Whether you've known for years that your family is flawed or you are just now finding out, there is hope. You were born into your family for a reason. God intends to use your experience, whether good or bad, to accomplish his purpose through you.

You may have scars that feel impossible to heal so you bury yourself in drugs and alcohol to dull the memories. Consider that while forgiveness and grace are an important part of Joseph's story, they are an important part of yours too. Maybe you need to have a little more grace and a whole lot more forgiveness with your family, not because they deserve it, but because it's time for you to move on.

Letting go doesn't mean you don't care. Far from it. Letting go means releasing your pain to God—who is the only one who can turn pain into promise—and running the race God has marked out for you. God can help you move on so you can move forward to be the person you want to be:

> *Therefore, since we are surrounded by such a great cloud of witnesses, let us throw off everything that hinders and the sin that so easily entangles. And let us run with perseverance the race marked out for us, fixing our eyes on Jesus, the pioneer and perfecter of faith. For the joy set before him he endured the cross, scorning its shame, and sat down at the right hand of the throne of God. Consider him who endured such opposition from sinners, so that you will not grow weary and lose heart. Hebrews 12:1-3 NIV*

Finally, if your family is especially toxic, please seek out further counseling. God can use your story for good, but sometimes it is healthy to get help setting boundaries. Forgiveness does not mean being a doormat. Forgiveness means releasing a hold someone has on you, and releasing someone from the hold you have on them.

Excuses, Excuses

The two main excuses I hear for hanging on to a Party Girl image are 1.) my friends will hate me; and 2.) Christians suck—they are all hypocrites. The first excuse is a shame because no real friend would dump you based on whether or not you experience a life change. The second is—well—sort of true and sort of not. Some Christians really are the worst. However, some are amazing. And as for being hypocrites, aren't we all? At any rate, both excuses are rooted in caring too much about what people think.

Excuse #1 My Friends Will Hate Me

Any true friend (Christian or not) will stick with you no matter what your drinking/sex convictions are. And, let's face it—your views on drinking and sex are usually the real issue, not whether or not you believe in God. Sometimes you find out that people you thought cared about you, don't. That hurts, but not nearly as much as you will hurt yourself trying to gain approval from other people. Be honest with your friends, "Hey, I am making some changes and figuring things out myself, but I still love you." Some people will support you, and some will probably reject you.

Ouch. The thought of friends making fun of you is painful. Backstabbing happens. It's ugly, but it happens. I can't imagine it feels good to be the person holding the knife either. Stand strong and remember that justice will prevail:

Do not fear the reproach of men or be terrified by their insults. For the moth will eat them up like a garment; the worn will devour them like wool. But my righteousness

will last forever, my salvation through all generations.
Isaiah 51:7b-8 NIV

Honesty is a great equalizer. When you choose to follow God, your behavior is likely to change. While you are in transition you may even over-correct your old ways becoming legalistic (aka someone obsessed with adhering to a bazillion rules in order to be a "good Christian") for a season. Either way, you get to find out what people really think about you. And that is good news because a fake friend is no friend at all. Fake friends will be revealed eventually anyway. You can love someone who doesn't support you but you don't have to be her best friend. **Turning the other cheek is not looking for abuse, but accepting that people feel differently and being okay with that.** Move on if you need to. And take time to find balance. A Christian is not someone who acts a certain way, but someone who trusts God with her whole life.

Keep your head held high. You can appreciate friendships, but idolizing them is a dangerous road. Crowds that once threw a parade and cheered for Jesus spit on Him and demanded His crucifixion a few days later. However, Jesus endured the scorn because He knew the truth. Jesus didn't let His popularity influence His mission, and He didn't hold the behavior of others against them either. In fact, Jesus' last words were "forgive them for they know not what they do." Instead of caring what your friends may or may not think, put your hope in a place that lasts:

Why am I discouraged? Why is my heart so sad? I will
put my hope in God! I will praise him again—my Savior
and my God! Psalm 42:5

Also—and I hope you find this encouraging—I had supportive great friends in high school, bad friends in college, and good friends now. Between the bad friends in college and now there was a period of transition that was lonely. But it didn't last forever and I'm so much better off. You can persevere. You really can. Praying for good friends and not settling for less is worth feeling lonely for a while. I promise.

In the meantime, don't be afraid to initiate new healthy friendships if you're old ones are fizzling out. Have you ever avoided texting a potential friend because—gulp—she might realize you're available? Me too. The first time I met my best friend Amy I thought she was way too nice to be friends with me (is that not the saddest thing?!? Don't think this way!). Everybody loved her, so I naturally assumed she was too busy to make time for me. I'm so glad I got over myself enough to admit I was worth having positive friends...and that I was not "too busy" to hang out either.

Excuse #2 Christians Suck— They are all Hypocrites...and Dorks

The first week of college a girl knocked on my dorm room door and invited me to a Bible study a couple of floors up. My crummy boyfriend was MIA, so I went. However, I sat strategically with my back to the hallway in case anyone I knew walked by. I don't remember who was there or what was said because of the huge, giant elephant in the room...the girl was wearing a crisp new pair of overall shorts. That's right. *Shorteralls.*

Thanks to her brand spanking new shorteralls—and my paranoia of what people thought of me—I had a revelation: Christians are dorks and I'd better not get caught dead with one. I reject the comeback of overalls for this very reason.

At work a year or so later, I met an outspoken, bubbly Christian girl I really liked. She didn't seem like a dork at all! In fact, I even hinted around that I would like to go to a campus ministry meeting with her. But she never took the bait, she never invited me. Instead, a bunch of co-workers went out one night and she was the only one who didn't drink—which she made sure we all knew. Thanks. That's super helpful. I felt like the bad guy in a public service announcement.

However, my life eventually soured to the point that—though it meant risking more judgment and walking into a campus ministry meeting alone—I went. The meeting went okay, but the super-involved ministry kids handed out lemonade to people as they dispersed from the auditorium, and...

TRAGEDY STRUCK.

Guess who handed me my lemonade? The bubbly girl. It was clear I was by myself. Out of self-preservation I decided to hate her forever. She was the dork, not me. And what was that business acting all nice after making me feel guilty the other night? Ugh, what a hypocrite.

Humiliated and wanting some validation, I walked straight to a house of a guy I knew liked me. A terrible guy. The only guy I knew who hated Christians way more than I did in that moment. He also did more drugs—both in variety and quantity—than anyone I had ever known. Supposedly he was a genius (way too smart to believe in God of course) and I knew I could count on him to make fun of the girl. Remember the list of things I'd tell myself at 20? He is #4. After graduation he worked at CVS where he was fired for stealing. Nice.

Judging people, and worrying about being judged yourself, is a slippery slope. I went from being paranoid someone would see me with Shorteralls to dating a drug addict with a penchant for cheesy crimes. I never meant for that to happen, but it did.

If my value as a person was based on what God thought of me 12 years ago, I never would've gone to that guy's house. I wouldn't have let a girl's outfit or the lack of an invite prevent me from finding a community of people who loved God and loved others. Honestly, I was quick to judge because I felt judged. I called people hypocrites because I was a hypocrite. Have you ever met someone who has never, not ever, been hypocritical? I haven't.

If you can't stand the group of Christians right in front of you, there's another group you will like...with or without overalls. Please-oh-please learn from my mistakes:

Not all Christians are dorks.

Over the past decade lots of girls have come and gone to the Bible study I hold at my house on Tuesdays. To be honest, they have been some of the most popular, successful students on campus. Some have been sorority presidents, UK homecoming queens, and student body officers. Some have been wild, some have been tame. Some have been funny, some have been serious. Some skip class constantly, some are destined for med school. Basically, not all Christians are dorks because not all Christians are the same.

What Happened to Grace Ann?

Despite living up to your party image because it's what people expect, despite growing up with memories you are trying to dull, despite your disappointment that the harder you try to make college the time of your life the more it sucks, you can change. You can!!

I love Grace Ann's story because she used to hide in the laundry room to avoid her roommate Ally who kept asking her to go to a campus ministry...but now she is spending a year working for that same organization! And even better, her story proves God is working behind the scenes whether you know it or not. When I told Grace Ann our Bible study prayed for her all last year as she hid in the laundry room, she teared up. She had no idea. Here is how God used Ally and Christian Student Fellowship (CSF), to change Grace Ann's heart:

> *Throughout this time (of partying), my sorority sister Ally had been relentlessly asking me to go with her to CSF. Eventually, after hitting my lowest point, I finally said yes and went with her one night. During worship I broke down. I cried during every song. Everyone there was so happy, and I finally realized how broken and lost I really was. I wanted to feel the genuine happiness that they felt. That was the moment I decided to explore Christianity.*
>
> *I will admit that I didn't do a 180 right then and there. I didn't fully give up my partying lifestyle right away. It was a slow, gradual change. I was learning. And God was so patient with me. By the end of my junior year I was a completely different person. I learned that God was unconditionally and deeply in love with me. I learned that He forgives ALL sins, and not only forgives, but*

FORGETS. I learned that He sent His son, Jesus Christ, into our world so that He could die for our sins. And most importantly, I learned that if you believe that Jesus Christ is the Son of God, and you accept Him into your heart, your sins are forgiven and you are A NEW CREATION.

A New Creation. I was broken, used, hurting and depressed. But God chased after me. Eventually I grew tired, and He outran me. He caught up to me and opened His arms to catch His broken Daughter. He made me new.

I was baptized on August 25, 2013. As I fell back into the water I could feel all of the dirtiness and sadness of my old life wash away. I came out of that water brand new. I could try to explain how happy my heart is now that I live for God, but words would never do it justice. Life is 100 times more beautiful now that I know Him. God took the most troubled girl and changed her from the inside out. God is my Father, my best friend and my strength.

No one is ever too lost or too far gone for God to find her. He will catch up with you every time. But if you take anything from my testimony, take this: stop running, or at least slow down. Because God has a true, unfailing love for you that far outweighs anything else in this life.

Now, Grace Ann still has fun. She kept all the fun-loving qualities she had before. After all, I'm not suggesting that if you go to a party you will go to Hell, but she likes herself the next day. It's okay to slow down and let yourself be loved. No matter how "far gone" you feel, it's important to distinguish fact from fiction. The fact is that if you put your complete trust in Jesus Christ, you are a valuable Daughter of God; the fiction is that your past actions will always define you.

Once a party girl, always a party girl does not have to be true of you. Besides, isn't it always a little sad to see someone my age trying to re-live the glory days? Do you really want to see me (a mid-thirties mother of two) in a tube top at your next fraternity party? Trust me, you don't. I'm grossed out just thinking about it.

Fake ID #2

Melody: The Perfectionist

My friend Melody is like a little sister to me—a much, much younger sister, but a sister nonetheless. She took a lot of the pictures for www.laneofroses.com last year. Not many people are allowed to pick up my kids from school, but Melody is. When we first met, I knew we would hit it off because we were both wearing the exact same opal necklaces, gifts from our grandmothers. Our connection was instant.

Melody is also extremely beautiful. Her picture is all over the Lane of Roses website so you can see for yourself (and if you are like me, I know you will!), but the interesting thing is that for a period of time her good looks nearly destroyed her. What started out as innocent—a few compliments on her appearance— turned into a full-blown eating disorder. A people pleaser by nature, Melody liked the positive attention of her initial weight loss but eventually confused her outside appearance with her worth. Her obsession was crippling. If she gained a few pounds, she felt like she was disappointing people. In her own words:

Somewhere in my childhood a lie crept in, and rooted itself deep in my heart—that lie being that my looks determined my worth. No matter how many times I heard that I shouldn't place my value in my outward appearance, it seemed as though the world around me was telling me the opposite. And so there I began to form my identity. Criticism from a close friend on my looks, words, and actions sent me down a path of crippling insecurity, and unhealthy friendships. The girl, whose worth had been built up on how she looked, didn't feel so pretty any more.

Once again...slowly but surely the self-doubt, fear of others' opinions, and insecurities crept back in. It moved fast, and I never meant to develop an eating disorder, but before I knew it I was a statistic. Another girl insecure and "dying to be thin..." The compliments on how good I looked were rolling in, and I thought I had everything under control. Which I did, for a little while...

But it became a daily battle. Every morning, the scale on my bathroom floor told me how I was going to feel about myself that day. I couldn't wait to weigh myself in the morning and see if I had lost another pound. I began keeping track of every single morsel that came into my mouth. Making it easy for me to cut out the "unnecessary" calories I was consuming. 90 calories for an apple, 200 for my half a sandwich, 60 for my grapes...so on and so on. The day I managed to consume only 400 calories for an entire day, I went to bed SO proud of myself. Everything was perfect, I was happy, and finally in control.

Confusing your inner worth with your outer appearance and performance is dangerous because you can't control either for any sustainable amount of time and be okay. Sooner or later, your greatest strength—tremendous willpower or the ability to perform well—transforms into your worst nightmare if you put too much stock into being The Perfectionist. No one looks perfect, acts perfect, achieves every imaginable goal, and is the best at everything all of the time.

No matter how tempting it is to define yourself as The Perfectionist, it is ultimately a Fake Identity. Looks and performance do not have anything to do with your Authentic Identity or value as a person. If you find perfection tempting, you have probably had some success with it. The problem is that no matter how good you look, or how successful you are, it will never be enough. There will always be someone who can out-perform you. Does that drive you crazy? What about knowing there is someone better looking, faster, smarter? Going nuts, yet? It doesn't have to be that way. You can get to a place of contentment and satisfaction, and actually enjoy being the real you. No strings attached.

PERFECTIONISM

When I was little, knowing that someone would always be better than me drove me insane. I wanted to be the best at everything in every way: the prettiest, smartest, the fastest, basically add"-est" to any word and that was my desire. Of course it came from a place of insecurity.

In 4th grade gym class I tied for dead last in the mile along with a girl who still ate her boogers. It was humiliating. I begged my mom to take me to the doctor because I was sure I had debilitating asthma, but the doctor said no. I was just out of shape.

Determined to never let this happen again, I began running compulsively. I would run all over our neighborhood and my eating habits became more and more peculiar. By the next year I discovered if I only ate once a day I could shed my baby fat a whole lot faster. My appearance changed fast, and I reveled in the attention. I felt vindicated. Finally people could see how amazing I really was and I was determined to never be in last place ever again. Ever. In anything.

Achieve, achieve, achieve, achieve. That's all I ever thought about. It's not like I had pushy parents either. They were great; it's just there was something in me that I hated—some weakness that I couldn't stand, but couldn't quite put my finger on. My self-loathing knew no bounds...and I was only in elementary school!

I was also obsessed with popularity (to which my mom asked the smartest two questions of all time: *How many popular kids are there?* Um, around 20. *Well, if only 20 out of 300 kids are popular, and 280 of those kids don't like the other 20, are they really popular?* This wasn't enough for me. Maybe it was the math.) My goal in life was to improve myself to the point I was better than the best—more popular than the most popular kid, smarter than the smartest, prettier than the prettiest, skinnier than the skinniest.

No matter how well I performed, I never achieved the perfection I craved. I always fell short. There is nothing in this world quite as agonizing as perfection because just when it seems within reach someone breezes along who can outperform you.

However, perfection is possible—conditionally, that is. Even the harshest critics of Jesus have to admit He was a pretty good guy, perfect even. If Jesus traded His life for yours, His superior qualities for your inferior ones, doesn't that make you perfect by association?

Yes. Yes it does. Through a relationship with Jesus Christ, His perfection covers your imperfection. You can finally take a deep breath and relieve yourself of the pressure of being the best. On your own, you never will be. However, you are not on your own. You can rely on the perfection of Jesus Christ and not your own performance for a sense of identity. When you mess up, you can release your mistakes to God and not beat yourself up for failing again.

God's love is made perfect in us. It's an internal thing, not performance-based:

> *No one has ever seen God; if we love one another, God abides in us and his love is perfected in us. 1 John 4:12 ESV*

Yet now he has reconciled you to himself through the death of Christ in his physical body. As a result, he has brought you into his own presence, and you are holy and blameless as you stand before him without a single fault.
Colossians 1:22

Paul is one of my favorite writers of all time. He wrote much of the New Testament after spending his earlier years murdering (murdering!) Christians. He was an over-achiever, a go-big-or-go-home type for sure. In fact, he grew up with the best of the best education and credentials and his goal in life was to out-achieve the best-achievers. Given his impressive lineage and education he had every opportunity to make that happen:

I am a Jew, born in Tarsus, a city in Cilicia, and I was brought up and educated here in Jerusalem under Gamaliel. As his student, I was carefully trained in our Jewish laws and customs. I became very zealous to honor God in everything I did, just like all of you today. And I persecuted the followers of the Way, hounding some to death, arresting both men and women and throwing them in prison. Acts 22:3,4

Despite Paul's sterling resume, he got confused. His background prepared him for success, but he found himself "hounding" Christians to death—which didn't feel so fulfilling after all. His obsession with maintaining Jewish law made a madman out of him. However, he noticed an important distinction between the law and his own motives:

So the trouble is not with the law, for it is spiritual and good. The trouble is with me, for I am all too human, a slave to sin. I don't really understand myself, for I want to do what is right, but I don't do it. Instead, I do what I hate. But if I know that what I am doing is wrong, this shows that I agree that the law is good. So I am not the one doing wrong; it is sin living in me that does it. Romans 7:14-17

Oh, Paul, how I can relate. The trouble is not my goals, it's with my heart. I started out wanting to be a better runner and improve my performance, and on my own my quest for perfection went awry. I wanted to do right, but I ended up doing things I hated when the pressure got too intense. My sin nature took over and controlled my life. There is a better way than achieving perfection on your own, but there is a catch. Seeking God's approval, not the approval of others, is the better choice.

You can't rely on perfection as the world defines it. After all, in Galatians 1:10 Paul says, "Am I now trying to win the approval of human beings, or of God? Or am I trying to please people? If I were still trying to please people, I would not be a servant of Christ. " When I try to please people, I feel stuck and anxious. But I don't have to stay that way:

But you are not controlled by your sinful nature. You are controlled by the Spirit if you have the Spirit of God living in you. (And remember that those who do not have the Spirit of Christ living in them do not belong to him at all.) And Christ lives within you, so even though your body will die because of sin, the Spirit gives you life because you have been made right with God. The Spirit of God, who raised Jesus from the dead, lives in you. And just as God raised Christ Jesus from the dead, he will give life to your mortal bodies by this same Spirit living within you. Romans 8:9-11

I don't have to earn perfection. God sees me through the lens of Jesus' perfection. He died for me knowing I'm screwed up and relieved me of the pressure of fixing myself. I can't fix myself. Thank goodness I don't have to. I can throw the goal of "be perfect" out the window because I don't have to *be* perfect, I *am* perfect through my relationship with God. He accepts me and covers my imperfections with the only perfect man, Jesus, who could offer a perfect life in trade for mine.

OBSESS MUCH?

By now it's surely clear that I can turn anything (a relationship, food, clothes, looks, *anything*) into an obsession. I used to think of an idol in a literal sense—a carved object or figurine—so I thought I was off the hook as far as idol worship goes. I mean, I do not have a statue on my mantel that I think will grant me wishes, so I must be good. However, I have come to realize that an idol can be absolutely anything I lean on more than God for comfort and fulfillment.

Let's use Melody's story as an example of how to tell when an object or situation turns into an obsession, or idol. Melody got some compliments on her looks. Her normal response was to enjoy the praise. Her out-of-balance response was to lean on that praise for her worth as a person…and obsessively count calories and take laxatives to keep the compliments rolling. She only felt good about herself if the number on the scale was exactly what she wanted it to be. Sometimes the line of obsession is hard to read, but it is important to maintain balance because an idol can rob us of peace and freedom.

Gripes. I don't want to admit this—especially since my sister-in-law is a teacher and she is helping me edit this thing—but I feel like I should. In high school I cheated in chemistry, geometry, and Spanish. There you have it. I flirted with nerds and taped cheat sheets in my calculator to get ahead.

Freshman year I was in the top 1% of my class, without cheating thank you very much. However, as my social commitments grew I didn't have the time to study and found myself slipping down the scale. Okay, okay, it wasn't just a lack of studying that made my grades drop…I also just plain suck at any and all left-brained activities. Geometry sophomore year was hard, but junior year chemistry was ten times worse. And as for Spanish, if you mumble the teacher can't tell what you're saying anyway so I never really knew any to start with. I just acted shy and wrote super messy on the tests.

Why did I cheat so much? I was obsessed with my straight A record. Grades *owned* me and knowing that I eventually had to cheat to get them made me feel dumb. For years after (and years and years and *years*) I was so insecure about my intelligence I missed out on some great opportunities; it's one reason it took me ten years to start this book. Now *that* is dumb. What might be dumber is my high school best friend's dad was our principal. Argh—my secret is out! Sorry, Jim.

How can you get rid of idols, or obsessions, in your own life?

1. **Admit it.** Call a spade a spade. If you absolutely cannot get over something, you might just be obsessed. When you're obsessed you miss out on the benefits of a relationship with God:

> *Those who cling to worthless idols forfeit the grace that could be theirs. Jonah 2:8 NIV*

2. **Pray.** Confess your obsession to God and seek accountability from a trustworthy friend to keep yourself in check. Remember:

> *The temptations in your life are no different from what others experience. And God is faithful. He will not allow the temptation to be more than you can stand. When you are tempted, he will show you a way out so that you can endure. 1 Corinthians 10:13*

3. **Cultivate an ongoing relationship with God.** He wants to be near to you, but if there is a big giant obsession in the way it can act as an obstacle blocking you from peace and contentment:

> *Come close to God, and God will come close to you. Wash your hands, you sinners; purify your hearts, for your loyalty is divided between God and the world. James 4:8*

> *I know what it is to be in need, and I know what it is to have plenty. I have learned the secret of being content in any and every situation, whether well fed or hungry, whether living in plenty or in want. I can do all this through him who gives me strength. Philippians 4:12, 13 NIV*

4. **Never give up.** If you truly give your obsession to God, that doesn't mean tempting thoughts won't cross your mind. Be prepared to override a tempting thought or lie with the truth. The truth will set you free. In fact, when you accept Christ, you are automatically freed—emphasis on the "d." Sometimes you just need to remind yourself that you already have freedom and that any bad thought is just that, a bad thought. There is no power in thoughts, good or bad, just distraction:

> *Never tire of doing right for at the proper time you will reap a harvest if you don't give up. Galatians 6:9 NIV*

> *Then you will know the truth, and the truth will set you free. John 8:32 NIV*

You can break free from your obsessive nature. In *Made to Crave*, Lysa Terkhuerst references Deuteronomy 2:3 NET "you've circled this mountain long enough; now turn north!" to remind her of her freedom. Despite witnessing miracle after miracle, the Israelites had little faith. Instead of claiming the promised land that was rightfully theirs, they wandered the desert for forty years. Finally, God told them to turn north and they found the land they craved. Deep down, what we crave is God. We can obsess about filling that void on our own, or we can turn north.

RELEASE CONTROL

(It's Not About You Anyway)

The first time someone said "Katie, it's not about you" (and I actually listened) was this past year. That explains a lot now that I think about it. I was 33 before I considered the world did not revolve around me. Anyhow, I was moaning and groaning about a million little things. Finally, the lady I was talking to said those magical five words, "Katie, it's not about you" and I haven't been the same since.

I decided to make "it's not about me" my theme song. Every time I obsessed about myself (it happens every four seconds if you're curious) I repeated the phrase "it's not about me" and moved on. It was hard at first because I had to say it 900 times a day, but eventually I began to change. Instead of trying to control my circumstances, I tried to remember it's not about me anyway (and I'm down to reminding myself only 300 times a day—progress!).

God didn't send Jesus to take on my sins and pain so that I can get everything I want all the time. I know! It shocked me too. He sent Jesus because He loves me, but more importantly to accomplish a vision bigger than one person who will be here and gone in the blink of an eye. We were created, not only for a loving relationship with God, but to bring Him glory. It's about HIM:

> *Bring all who claim me as their God, for I have made them for my glory. Isaiah 43:7*

The other week our pastor (Jon Weece, www.southlandchristian.org) was saying that glory means weight in the original language. When we give glory to God we are releasing a weight off our shoulders and on to His. That blows my mind.

One of my favorite chapters in the whole Bible is Psalm 23. Yes, it is mostly read at funerals, but whenever I'm depressed it always makes me feel better. Verse 3 says "He guides me down the right paths, for His name's sake." Notice it doesn't say "He guides me down the right paths, for *my* sake." God guides me, not to make me happier, but to bring honor to His own name. It's not about me; it's about God. Giving God fame, honor, recognition, and weight is the point of why any of us are here.

Knowing life is not all about me is freeing because whenever I'm obsessed about myself I'm a discontented train wreck. The more I focus on myself, the more I try to control my circumstances, the more miserable I become. Ironically, the fruit of thinking more about God is joy and peace.

In John 14:12 Jesus says, "You can ask for anything in my name, and I will do it, so that the Son can bring glory to the Father." Again, the point is bringing glory to the Father. And Jesus is our model. If His motivation was to glorify God, then ours should be the same.

Another way of bringing glory or attention to God is worship. And worshipping does not necessarily mean singing old hymns in church. It can, but it certainly isn't the only way. Thank goodness because while I love to listen to great singers, I am not one of them. I mouth the word *watermelon* over and over to make it look like I'm singing (thanks, Dad. Best advice ever).

Worshipping God means offering *everything* to Him—not hanging on to a piece of your life (your boyfriend, your success, your appearance) that you don't quite trust Him to manage and want to control on your own. As our love response to *His* love, God wants all of us. He wants us to hold every area of our lives— our money, our relationships, our activities—in open hands.

So often, if something is important to me I hang on to it with a death grip. My biggest act of worship occurs when I say, "God, it's not about me. I'm releasing this part of my life to you because you love me and I love you." Besides, whenever I clutch on to something too tightly I eventually suffocate what's in my hands. Ultimately, God knows what is best for us and has the power to make good plans happen.

Your role in understanding your identity is to acknowledge God as Creator and Savior and love Him back. I used to think my role as a Christian was to follow rules perfectly. When I succeeded, I thought I was awesome. But when I failed, I was a loser. I just didn't get it.

Although I'm getting way more balanced, I still occasionally vacillate between two extremes: thinking I'm the Worst Person Ever vs. thinking I'm the Best Person Ever. Neither is really accurate, and both ways of thinking are self-focused. I am capable of terrible behavior—that is absolutely true. However, who I am is not necessarily how I act in a moment of weakness. Similarly, just because I make a great decision and feel confident in a certain moment doesn't mean I should be the Supreme Ruler of the Universe either. Besides, it's just not about me.

A while ago I got my first hate mail from www.laneofroses. com. Until that fateful email, all of the other responses had been super encouraging. Whenever I got one, I would be on a high for hours. Until one night I checked my email as I headed out the door...and it was bad. My husband and I were supposed to be on a rare overnight date night, but after I read the scathing email I was miserable.

After a couple hours of sitting across from a teary and preoccupied wife, Anthony said the smartest thing I'd ever heard. He said if I was absorbing the negative words from that one email, then I was absorbing the praise as well. Shouldn't I reflect *everything*—the good and the bad—to God? If I put my value in what people think, I'm screwed. Some people will always hate me, some people will always (well, to my face anyway) love me. Even my opinion of myself changes fifty times a day depending on my mood.

Hebrews 13:8 says "Jesus Christ is the same yesterday, today, and forever." He doesn't change and He loves you. In order to see myself accurately, I need to remember my value is in the hands of an unchanging God. He loves me the same yesterday, today and forever.

Now, when someone gives me a compliment, I give God the praise. When someone rips me a new one, I cast my worries on Him. **Reflect the praise and deflect the insults.** It doesn't matter what people think, it matters what God thinks. Give it all—the praise, the insults—to God. After all, God's the boss. And it's not about me anyway.

What Happened to Melody?

It's funny how perfectionism makes me feel anything but perfect. Instead control, obsession, and pressure to be the best make me feel inferior. Here is what Melody has learned about her identity:

One night, lying in my dorm room, I was crying in my bed as I did most nights. And after years of going back and forth with God, this night was my turning point. I finally let go. I decided to give it all up to God. My relationships, my disorder, my life, everything. I couldn't believe any of those words came out of my mouth. I couldn't believe I was releasing control. My boyfriend and I ended our relationship shortly after that night. It was awful, and I was heartbroken. But I've never learned more than I did in this season of my life.

I'm not going to say I did everything right after that, or that everything was a piece of cake after that one prayer. But over the next few years my heart began to heal. I slowly overcame hurdles with food, body image, exercise, relationships, and friendships. Finding a Christ-like community at a campus ministry was one of the best things I ever did. They showed me the Lord's heart, how to love, detect lies from the devil, and how to view myself as an amazing strong woman of God. I was refreshed with an eagerness to learn anything I could about my God; a Father who took a burden that was at times far too heavy for me to carry.

I love you, Melody. You really are a new person made perfect through Christ. The pressure is off. Even though you are super talented and wonderful, you don't let the pressure to be *more* talented or *more* wonderful wreck you. You are strong. You are changed. You are perfect because that's how God sees you through your relationship with Him.

Fake ID #3

Erika: The Girlfriend

Geez. I don't know about you, but when Erika admitted, "I was in a crappy relationship with a guy I didn't even like that much" she summed up about 5 whole years of my life. Erika is in a sorority at UK, and is one of the regular contributors on www.laneofroses.com. If I only had one and only one word to describe her it would be "cool." She's fun, energetic, self-deprecating, and a sports-fanatic with a raspy voice. Boys want to date her and girls want to be her friend. But who cares what I think? When it comes to Erika's identity it doesn't matter what I see, it matters how she feels...and even then that's not enough. Here is Erika's experience in her own words:

I've spent my whole life on a search: I've been searching for attention, for love, for acceptance, for affirmation. Mostly, I've been on a search for an identity for myself...

Growing up, I went to a Catholic grade school and high school, which, for me, translated to studying God but not really knowing Him. I didn't really think about God much; why would I? He was God, up in the sky making rules, and I was me, wandering around down here breaking them. I was a punk of a child, I tested my parents nerves daily so what I did know about God was that He probably didn't like me too much anyways. No matter. I didn't even really care what people thought. I mean, I did, but in my mind it was me vs. them. My heart used to be barricaded by anger; anger at my life, at the people in it, and at a god I didn't know or understand. This anger led to a lot of negative consequences and poor decisions when I was growing up.

I thought that I would finally be happy if everyone liked me; I was such a people pleaser. However, this became dangerous when I didn't care what kind of people I was pleasing just as long as I had friends. I found my self-worth completely in others' opinions of me. By my junior year of high school, this had me focusing on boys and alcohol and all kinds of dumb things I shouldn't have been doing. I was a mess. I didn't like myself at all but had no idea how to change. I'll paint this picture for you: it's towards the end of my junior year, I had lost a lot of good friends. I had just been busted by my parents for drinking. I had recently totaled my car. I was in a crappy relationship with a guy I didn't even like that much. And I was going on a weekend retreat that was required by school. This was going to be good. Not.

Seeking "The Girlfriend" identity is a common trap for us all; I've been there and I promise I've seen this one trip up more girls than I could possibly count. Defining yourself based on what a guy, or guys, think can lead to a lot of pain because in the end it is a Fake Identity.

There is no lasting joy or peace found in being the object of some Joe Schmoe's affection. Even if you do get married—and remember I've been married for a decade so roll with me here—

you can't define yourself based on your husband's opinion of you. People change, people make mistakes, and no one is ever perfect.

Even the best husband in the world will disappoint you at some time or another...and you will disappoint him too. What Anthony thinks of me matters, but it doesn't define me—I'm not the perfect wife, and I don't have to be. Thank goodness, because when we got married we divvied up household jobs and I suck at most of mine. I've molded countless loads of laundry by accident. Here's a nickel's worth of free advice: Don't leave wet clothes in the washing machine for five days. It rots.

Boys, Boys, Boys

The reason I can relate so much to Erika is because in college (alright, it started like in kindergarten) I was super paranoid of never landing a husband and thought about boys all of the time. And I mean *all-of-the-time.* I know that's not very progressive of me, but it's the truth. I wasted so much time fretting over whether or not I would get married. *What ifs* constantly raced through my mind. In fact, my thoughts typically went something like this:

> *What if no one wants to marry me??!!! What if I already met him but missed my chance? What if my future husband cheats on me someday? Oh no! I thought it so now it will come true...*

The *what ifs* did not stop there. There's a million more where that came from. What a waste. I didn't meet my husband until after college anyway.

Single (and living in the downright panicky fear of staying that way) I wanted to let go of the obsession but didn't know how. It took a scary stalker-esque experience with an ex-boyfriend to finally make me throw my hands in the air and say "I give up! A rotten boyfriend is way worse than no boyfriend at all!" To avoid learning the hard way—or to let go of your own weirdo of a boyfriend—here are some tips on how to break free from defining yourself as "The Girlfriend" at all...

But really, who am I kidding? First things first. Last semester a group of sorority girls (accomplished, motivated, successful sorority girls at that) were on my front porch and someone asked, "What's your biggest fear?" No kidding, the answer for each and every one of them was "Not getting married and having kids." And, before you dismiss me because I'm from Kentucky, please know that I met for hours with a super ambitious girl from *Connecticut* who said the same thing!! It is just a fact. A lot of girls fear not getting married and having kids—which may just be another way of expressing an even deeper fear...the fear of being alone.

If you can't bear the thought of being alone, here is what you should do:

#1 Embrace Being Single!!

Although it sounds counterintuitive, this is the most important step. And it's the step girls ask me about the most! Lately, I've heard from all sorts of girls trying to be patient and not freak out about being single when all their friends seem to have boy-friends...or even more frustrating, fiancés or brand new hus-bands. Jerks.

Odds are you eventually will be in a relationship, so it makes sense to devote your time to learning your God-given gifts and interests. When you're in a relationship, it's easy to trick yourself into thinking you like something just because the other person does. For example, I didn't mean to tell bold-faced lies when I was dating my husband, but I was so blinded by how much I enjoyed his company I convinced myself I liked activities that I hate (fast motorcycle rides, adventurous travels to foreign lands with no planning or hotel accommodations, the list goes on and on... and on).

Being single is a gift—a gift you may not want—but a gift nonetheless. Instead of obsessing about "being alone" realize that some of the loneliest people are married. Being married will not solve all your problems or ease all your fears. Did you hear that? *Being married will not solve all your problems or ease all your fears.* It won't. In fact, it can make things a whole lot worse if you marry the wrong person.

I was telling one of my girls the other day that she could have a ring on her finger in three months or less if she really wanted... but was that what she really wanted? Manipulate some guy to propose then spend the rest of your life regretting it? Forget that. Embrace the time you have to get to know God and yourself better.

In many ways I'm living the dream—great husband, cute kids—but man, a great husband and cute kids are *work.* No one ever bothered telling me that; or if anyone did, I didn't listen. It will be 2070 before I get to do whatever I want, whenever I want. My former pet peeve, ragged fingernails with chipped paint, has become my reality. But doing anything about my nails doesn't make the cut on my list of priorities. I have to make choices now, both large and small, that I didn't have to when I was single.

This might be your last chance to do what you want to do for a long time. Live it up:

> *...a woman who is no longer married or has never been married can be devoted to the Lord and holy in body and in spirit. But a married woman has to think about her earthly responsibilities and how to please her husband. 1 Corinthians 7:34*

By the way "how to please her husband" can be an "earthly responsibility" that will totally wear you out. Sex is absolutely, positively great. Heck, it might be the only thing on your mind now. But when you can have it whenever you want it, it's easy to take it (and your husband) for granted. Sometimes as a mom you will be so tired tears stream down your face out of sheer exhaustion. You're not sad, you're just sooo tired. Eventually, you will come around and feel human again, but when your kids are little, the most appealing part of "sleeping together" is sleeping.

You can say it won't happen to you, but talk to me in ten years. It happens. Every mom that bought this book as a high school graduation gift and is secretly reading this on her own is smiling to herself right now. Just you wait.

So for today, write down 5 things about your life that if they were gone tomorrow you would really miss. Life does not have peaks and valleys. It is a railroad track—two parallel lines—of good experiences on one side and bad ones on the other. Whenever you are thinking too much about bad stuff all you really need to do is look to the other side. Remember there is always a good rail too. The good parts of being single: reading a book in the tub, painting your nails whenever you want, meeting your friends on a whim (or having friends at all!), going on a run whenever you feel like it, *not* having to hang out with your boyfriend's lame roommates, are a luxury you will someday miss. I promise.

#2 Don't Date Losers

That's my spin on my sister-in-law's quote "never date someone you wouldn't marry." I am lucky because I did land one heck of a husband, but I kissed a few frogs first. However, contrary to what you may have heard, you absolutely do NOT have to kiss a bunch of frogs before finding your prince. You just don't.

One of the biggest, fattest lies out there is "all guys are the same." Not true! There are some great guys out there!!! If you aren't meeting any nice guys, you might be running in the wrong circles. Ask yourself "is this a guy I want to father my children?" and if the answer is "Gross!!! Never!!!" head for the hills as fast as you possibly can. Run—don't walk—from a bad relationship. If a guy is not someone you would want to marry, don't hook up with him. You might get stuck.

There are too many great guys out there to settle for a manipulative jerk…or even to settle for someone who isn't a loser, but is just filling up a spot until you meet the right guy. That's not fair to anyone, especially the nice guy who thinks you like him when you really don't.

Wondering if you need to head for the hills? If the following descriptions remind you of your relationship, it might not be a relationship worth having:

1. **You secretly can't stand him.** Seriously, if he gets on your last nerve now, it will only get worse. Get out now while you still can.

2. **He embarrasses you.** I was so embarrassed by one guy I dated that after I introduced him to someone, I whispered "I'm so sorry, I'm so sorry" behind his back to whatever poor soul had just met him. Do you really want to have to admit this one day like I am now?

3. **You can't stand yourself when you're with him.** He should bring out the best in you and vice versa. One girl I know has been with a royal a-hole for so many years, she's kind of mean now too. Now, when I see her walking my way I duck behind a pole to avoid her death glare. Sad.

4. **You fight like cats and dogs.** If you fight when you're dating, you'll fight like cats and dogs when you're married. Do you really want to be in a grudge match your whole life?

5. **His character sucks.** Be realistic. If he watches porn 24-7, is super lazy, and does drugs all day it doesn't matter if he's

popular in his fraternity. Bad character is bad character no matter how good of a catch a guy appears to the rest of the world (*but he's from a good family, but he's popular, but he's rich, but I'm so lucky he noticed me...*Gag. You're better than that!)

6. **He criticizes you constantly**. From the way you breathe to the way you spell your name, he nit-picks every little thing about you.

7. **He would be a horrible father.** My husband just took my little girl to a daddy/daughter dance and it made her so happy I cried. More often than not, you get to choose the father of your kids. Make it a man who will take her to a daddy/daughter dance. You won't regret it.

8. **He's a project.** If you think "well, if I change X, Y, and Z he'll be alright" you need to bolt, for your sake and his. You are no magician. You can't magically change anyone no matter how persuasive you are.

9. **Everyone you know hates him**. Your friends and family might be seeing something obvious that some insecurity or blindness on your part is preventing you from seeing clearly.

10. **Your values don't line up.** Oh boy, this is a biggie. You might be able to bite your tongue about your beliefs while you date, but you will eventually have to make decisions based on what you believe is right.

If I just described your boyfriend and you want to make a change but don't know how, the next step is for you.

#3 Break Free From a Bad Relationship

In case, you're not struggling with being single, but struggling with being in a relationship that sucks, I hear you. Interestingly,

I struggled with both extremes in a short period of time. In other words, you'll find no judgment here. Just support. However, there is a verse I would like to point out that I find completely awesome:

> *Of them the proverbs are true: "A dog returns to its vomit,"*
> *and, "A sow that is washed returns to her mud." 2 Peter 2:22*

In college I would either feel too bad to break up with someone or I would break up with someone only to get back together 10 million times...like a dog returning to its vomit! Ha! I really did! Both were unhealthy scenarios, and just when I finally thought I had created a perfect system (I would act bored and mean until the other person broke up with me) I realized it had flaws too.

Some relationships are hard to end because the boyfriend has so embedded himself in your life it's really hard to let go. I might just know this from experience. If you're not being respected or valued as a person, you just might be in an unhealthy relationship. Here are my tips on how to break free:

1. Run! Hide! Change your name and join a convent! Kidding... unless that's what it takes.

2. Identify whether or not a relationship needs ending; check out the list above for a clue. Is this a healthy relationship? Ask yourself: Am I valuing my boyfriend as a person and does he value me? Does this person bring out the best in me or the worst in me?

3. If you have tried without success to end an unhealthy relationship (you keep getting back together with someone out of loneliness, insecurity, or the person simply will NOT go away...or let's be honest, maybe it's you that won't go away), here are some ideas to make the break easier:

   a. Make some new, encouraging friends! It's easier to distance yourself from a boyfriend if you have a fun social outlet. Just make sure the friends are constructive, and not part of the problem.

b. Seek relationship advice from your parents or someone older than you that has the type of life you would like to have. If someone older thinks the relationship is bad news, it probably is. Odds are a caring older-than-you person would love to help keep you accountable to ending a bad relationship.

c. If your relationship was isolating enough, you may not have a good friend right now. Don't let embarrassment prevent you from reaching out for help. You are not the only person to cling to a boyfriend so tightly he becomes the only person in your life. If need be, call a counselor (a trustworthy Christian counselor) and get some professional advice pronto. There are reputable counseling websites listed on www.laneofroses.com.

Remember above all that you are loved and valued by God— no matter what your boyfriend thinks! God loves you, and according to Jeremiah 29:11 NIV, has "plans to prosper you…to give you hope and a future." Don't settle for anything less. God may have an even better plan for you, so don't get so caught up in controlling all of the details of your future (because you can't) or forcing relationships to work out that would be better left alone. Maybe God is preparing the perfect guy for you; maybe He has another adventure in store. No matter what, you can trust that God is good. His plans are good.

For now, try replacing your chain of anxiety-inducing *what ifs* (and other lies) with more constructive thoughts:

That is why we never give up. Though our bodies are dying, our spirits are being renewed every day. For our present troubles are small and won't last very long. Yet they produce for us a glory that vastly outweighs them and will last forever! So we don't look at the troubles we can see now; rather, we fix our gaze on things that cannot be seen. For the things we see now will soon be gone, but the things we cannot see will last forever. 2 Corinthians 4:16-18

You are blessed because you believed that the Lord would do what he said. Luke 1:45

The temptations in your life are no different from what others experience. And God is faithful. He will not allow the temptation to be more than you can stand. When you are tempted, he will show you a way out so that you can endure. 1 Corinthians 10:13

Submit yourselves, then, to God. Resist the devil (or a crappy boyfriend), and he will flee from you. James 4:7 NIV—emphasis mine

#4 Be Honest With Yourself

While there are some great guys out there, a lot of guys do use girls for their own selfish gain. They'll sleep with girls they don't care about just to satisfy their own urges and believe it's okay. They'll lie, criticize, manipulate, and abuse—anything to keep you down so that you won't think you're good enough to do better. Girls, you're way too valuable to waste your time with someone who doesn't appreciate your worth.

God made you exactly the way He wants you; He does not make mistakes. If you can relate to Erika's confession of being "in a crappy relationship with a guy I didn't even like that much" you can make a change. YOU ARE VALUABLE. When you honor the person God created you to be, you will attract the kind of spouse that honors you as well.

As someone who finally hit the relationship jackpot, take it from me—you want to spend your life with someone who honors you. It is soooo worth holding out for an awesome husband if a husband is what you really desire. Proverbs 37:4 says "Take delight in the LORD, and he will give you the desires of your heart." I don't think this means God is a genie that gives you whatever you want, but when it comes to whether or not you "deserve" a good guy? You do. Hold. Out. For. This. You are worth it. It is worth it. Have faith and patience that God has a plan for you and that he has a plan for your future husband too.

If you can't be content with your current circumstances you won't be content later anyway. Your worth as a person relies on what GOD thinks of you, not whether or not you have a boyfriend. A guy may make you feel like you're dime a dozen, or even tell you that's what you are. But God custom-designed you, you're beautiful and unique.

God's plans are good and always worth the wait; and getting your satisfaction from God is always a good thing. Embrace being single, don't settle for a bad relationship, and don't worry about the future, enjoy today!!!!

There's No Such Thing as Damaged Goods

One of the reasons I've seen girls, and myself, cling to a crappy relationship is feeling like it's the best she can do. If your boyfriend keeps you around with the 1 nice thing he does to make up for the 10 bad ones, the way you see yourself is askew.

My senior year of college I remember walking home from class thinking, "I don't deserve my boyfriend. After the things I've done, I can't believe he would be with a person like me." I did whatever that boyfriend wanted me to do—cut off all other social connections, spent every waking second waiting for his call—because my value as a person hinged on his opinion of me.

No Friends + Constant Negative Self-talk + Controlling Boyfriend= Bondage. There is a better way, but you have to choose to see yourself how God sees you first.

If you are feeling ashamed about relational choices you have made (or have your own tape of crazy thoughts running through your mind) consider this: Jesus Christ Himself had a prostitute grandma. He also had a widow, cheating wife (or rape victim depending on how you look at it), and other regular, everyday women in His lineage. I love it!!! The family history shows that God is a champion of women...and not one of us has to be perfect to make a difference.

Billions of lives have been restored because Jesus offers hope and freedom, and God used ordinary women to accomplish His extraordinary purpose. In Jesus day, lineage was crucial to identity. It was no small deal that women were even mentioned at all in the family history of Jesus. Back then, women were usually just left out. Check out the lives of the women below, either google them or look up the passages, and be encouraged!! No matter what your past looks like, God can use your circumstances or choices for good:

☑ Rahab, the prostitute- Joshua 2; 6:17

☑ Ruth, the widow- Ruth 1: 4:13-17

☑ Bathsheba, forced to cheat- 2 Samuel 11; 12:15, 18, 24

☑ Mary, the unwed mother- Luke 1:26

(For a complete list of all the women mentioned in Jesus' lineage, look up Matthew 1:1-17)

Also, consider the story in John 8 of a woman who was caught in the act of adultery. The powerful religious leaders, the Pharisees, forced her to stand before the temple courts (like the busy center of downtown during lunch hour) and tried to get Jesus to throw stones at her. Instead, Jesus said "Let any one of you who is without sin be the first to throw a stone at her." Afterwards, the crowd dispersed and Jesus asked the woman, "Woman, where are they? Has no one condemned you?" "No one, sir," she said. "Then neither do I condemn you," Jesus declared. "Go now and leave your life of sin."

Straight from the mouth of Jesus Christ, don't let your imperfect choices prevent you from a healing relationship with God. You are loved by God, no matter what your sexual track record looks like. As a beloved Daughter of God, it breaks His heart to see you settling for an unhealthy relationship. Make a choice to turn from old (or current!) mistakes to God who desires what's best for you.

Examples of God's grace are scattered everywhere in the Bible. Please know you are loved:

So now there is no condemnation for those who belong to Christ Jesus. And because you belong to him, the power of the life-giving Spirit has freed you from the power of sin that leads to death. Romans 8:1, 2

Even if you decide right now that—yes, you are valuable— only to mess up later on, don't beat yourself up. Making mistakes doesn't mean you are a mistake, or a loser. It means you're human. Change happens when you realize you *are changed* through faith. Jesus changed you—as in the change is finished, past tense, it's over. You are changed and the more you understand that the more your behavior and thoughts will adjust. It will take time. You will mess up, but if you continue to pursue a close relationship with God it will be okay. You will be okay.

What Happened to Erika?

What I love about Erika is her vulnerability. Despite clinging to a relationship for validation in the past, this is how she sees herself now:

> I finally met this guy Jesus I had been reading about in textbooks my whole life and, to my surprise, He didn't hate me. He didn't think I was worthless like I had convinced myself I was. He hadn't given up on me. For the first time ever, I was shown love without limits or conditions. It was the most freeing experience of my life. Looking back on that time in my life, the grace and gentle love God showed me along the way is mind-blowing. Here I was in the middle of this free fall while my life was unraveling around me and right before I hit rock bottom, the Lord's hand reached out and caught me.

> ...He showed me with great love that His opinion was the only one that mattered and that as long as I am His child, I am as perfect as I'll ever be. He reminded me again and again that I am fearfully and wonderfully made (Psalm 139) and that He has made me righteous by Jesus' death on the cross and nothing I can ever do will beat that...

> ...And this, finally, is the identity I've spent my life so desperately searching for: that I am the Daughter of a King, I'm His beloved princess. I'm incredibly humbled by the grace and goodness God has shown me in the long time it took for me to embrace Him completely. He has been patient with me in every identity I failed to find fulfillment in and He has been my strength on my worst days. He has been peace in my anxiety and my closest friend. There's a verse in Acts that is about Paul being trapped at sea, but I never think of that when I read it and it is one of my favorites in the whole Bible. It reads: "I gave way and let myself be driven." Giving way of myself

*and my fears and anxieties has allowed God to totally
free me and drive me to the person He created me to be.*

You, like Erika, don't have to base your worth based on being
some guy's girl. You're worth so much more than that—and you
are some guy's girl. That "some guy" is God and, unlike that
dummy who keeps forgetting your birthday, He has no flaws.

Fun, perfect performance, and relationships—oh boy,
relationships—never satisfied any of us. Not Grace Ann, not
Melody, not Erika, and especially not myself. Searching for
validation in any of these areas never worked because there was
no real validation to be found. They were Fake IDs. Fake ways of
defining ourselves that left us wanting, lacking, thirsty for more.

Sure, tips and advice on how to avoid any of the Fake IDs
are great. But figuring out who you don't want to be and places
where you don't want to anchor your identity isn't enough. If
you aren't fake, and don't want to settle for fake, you have to
define what's real.

An Authentic Identity is possible. And more fulfilling,
rewarding, and exciting than I ever imagined.

Part 3

AUTHENTIC IDs

What is an Authentic Identity?

Seeing Yourself as God Sees You

Dear Young Katie,

I would love to scoop you up in a hug and assure you it will be okay. But you would just push me away, roll your eyes, and cuss me out to prove you're doing just fine.

Now that I think about it, you're kind of a butthole right now. But that's okay. I know you have your reasons. You're not mean, you're lost. It hurts.

What I want you to know is that God loves you.** He loves you like a daughter. He loves you like a very best friend. He loves you like a groom loves his bride. **He loves you, He loves you, He loves you.

You are not disposable. You don't have to try so hard. And you don't have to wait until you are good enough for God to accept you. He already has.

You can be secure because you are loved securely.

Love,

Your Medium Old Self

The point of figuring out who you really are is NOT to merely get by or survive. No way! There is no need to settle for a ho-hum life, avoiding the Fake IDs but never really living. But since ho-hum might seem better than being downright miserable, you might be okay with that. Don't be.

A relationship with God frees you to live out your full potential. You can thrive! No more getting by and surviving for you! Whatever Fake IDs have tripped you up or knocked you down in the past—boys, looks, perfection—you get a do-over. You get a fresh start and a chance to find out who you really are and what you really like. If you put your faith in Christ, you can discover your Authentic Identity. You are no longer confined to being The Girlfriend, Life of the Party, or Perfectionist. You are a New Creation:

> *This means that anyone who belongs to Christ has become a new person. The old life is gone; a new life has begun! 2 Corinthians 5:17*

Your Authentic Identity is your Identity in Christ. Simply put, "Identity in Christ" is seeing yourself as God sees you. When you put your faith in Him, your old insecurities don't have to control you anymore. The power of Christ lives in you. *In Christ* means your sins were crucified on the cross, and you trust Him to give you strength, focus, and purpose:

> *My old self has been crucified with Christ. It is no longer I who live, but Christ lives in me. So I live in this earthly body by trusting in the Son of God, who loved me and gave himself for me. Galatians 2:20*

All the baggage of a New Creation is g-o-n-e gone. The past is in the past. You don't have to worry anymore:

> *Give all your worries and cares to God, for He cares about you. 1 Peter 5:7*

Not only can you give your worries to God, He will fight your battles for you. You don't have to overcome anything on your own:

This is what the LORD says: Do not be afraid! Don't be discouraged by this mighty army, for the battle is not yours, but God's. 2 Chronicles 20:15b

A life with God is not all hype; He follows through. I was so disappointed when college was not the time of my life. All the stuff I thought would be so fun brought me nothing but pain. I never meant for that to happen, but it did. However, life with God has been the adventure of a lifetime that continues to exceed my wildest expectations. I still get giddy and teary-eyed about my New Creation identity!

God sees me based on my potential. He sees who I *can* be— not my current state of being or how I see myself in the here and now. I tend to lump my mistakes or choices in with who I am, but He sees me as perfect through the sacrifice of Jesus: perfect and capable of great things.

This is exactly what Erika, Melody, Grace Ann, and I are learning. We are New Creations, and the baseline for our identity is love. Nothing—no horrible circumstance, no critical person, no overwhelming day—can separate us from God's love either. Finally, we are secure:

No power in the sky above or in the earth below- indeed, nothing in all creation will ever be able to separate us from the love of God that is revealed in Christ Jesus our Lord. Romans 8:31

And last but not least, it's not about me anymore! The more I tried to define myself, enjoy myself, reward myself, motivate myself—the more I focused on myself in general—

the gloomier I became. Living for God is liberating because my focus has shifted. I get it now. God made me to give honor to His name, not mine. Turns out, the root cause for so much of my past bondage was selfishness.

Ironically though, before understanding *who I am* I have to understand *who God is*. After all, how I see God is a reflection of how I see myself.

One of the girls recently wrote a sweet blog post about her older sister. She said her sister was the most important person in her life and is the reason for her "over-confidence." Her sister was always so encouraging she felt like she could conquer the world. But what if the most important person in your life is discouraging instead? Does that mean you're insecure, lacking confidence? Sometimes.

What happens when God is the most important person in your life? Are you automatically confident and worry-free? Not necessarily. It depends on how you perceive Him.

I used to feel like God was watching my every move like a hawk. Not in a fatherly, protective way but in a mean waiting-for-me-to-screw-up kind of way. So it's really no surprise I was way too hard on myself.

When I was in middle school, a youth group at another church had the kids write down the names of people in our class who appeared to be Christians based on their actions. My name came up as one of the "Christian-acting" kids. It made my parents really proud, but to me it felt like an enormous burden. What if I lost my spot? Better act perfect all the time. Other kids were watching. Pressure, pressure, pressure.

I eventually cracked. My natural assumption was that God was scrutinizing my every move too. After all, isn't that what the kids in the middle school youth group were doing? Sheesh, what a way to take a compliment. Complete paranoia and an identity crisis. I'm pretty sure the other kids never thought twice about that list ever again.

Part of my demise was my morning pep talk ritual. I stared at my reflection every morning and recited the following:

Alright you stupid turd. What is up with your hair?! Ugh. You can do better. Treat every day like it's picture day. No slacking. Be extra nice. Oh, and tell people you're happy because you go to church. Dammit.

I do not recommend these little pep talks.

However, it *is* possible to quit believing lies about yourself. But you have to learn how to recognize a lie first.

How you see God is often how you see yourself, and you have a real live enemy who is trying to prevent you from seeing God's true character. I didn't know that. I'd heard of Satan of course, but I sort of thought of him as an abstract, scary theory or cartoon character with a red tail and pitchfork—not a real personal threat.

I judged myself severely, hated myself when I screwed up, and sometimes just putting one foot in front of the other was hard— way too hard. No wonder! For crying out loud, I looked in the mirror and told myself how much I sucked every morning. I made a point of repeating lies to myself every morning because I didn't know they were lies. I thought I was being realistic, helpful even. However, I have learned to separate fact from fiction, truth from lies.

My pastor says that if you believe the first line of the Bible "In the beginning God created the heavens and the earth" then the rest is easy to believe. For some, it's easy to believe in God, but weird to believe in the devil as well. Unfortunately, Satan is real and it's important to recognize his lies. **God loves, guides, and delivers; Satan hates, tricks, and deceives:**

The thief comes only to steal and kill and destroy. I came that they may have life and have it abundantly. John 10:10 ESV

Jesus was accosted by misguided religious leaders several times. They couldn't and wouldn't believe Jesus was the Messiah, and chose to believe Satan's lies over God's truth. In their minds, the predicted Messiah would come with a sword and a vengeance and they refused to believe Jesus despite the predictions He fulfilled:

Jesus told them, "If God were your Father, you would love me, because I have come to you from God. I am not here on my own, but he sent me. Why can't you understand what I am saying? It's because you can't even hear me! For you are the children of your father the devil, and you love to do the evil things he does. He was a murderer from the beginning. He has always hated the truth, because there is no truth in him. When he lies, it is consistent with his character; for he is a liar and the father of lies. John 8:42-44

The Father of Lies is the perfect title for Satan. Hindsight is 20/20 because looking back I believed terrible lies about myself. I was a lost cause, could never measure up. However, God is love, and He sent His Son to die to restore a relationship with me. How could I doubt the character of God? Because Satan is sneaky:

Stay alert! Watch out for your great enemy, the devil. He prowls around like a roaring lion, looking for someone to devour. 1 Peter 5:8

However, sneaky as Satan may be, he is a defeated foe. He can lie to you, yes, but you have the power to overcome those lies through faith in Christ:

A final word: Be strong in the Lord and in his mighty power. Put on all of God's armor so that you will be able to stand firm against all strategies of the devil. For we are not fighting against flesh-and-blood enemies, but against evil rulers and authorities of the unseen world, against mighty powers in this dark world, and against evil spirits in the heavenly places. Ephesians 6:10-12

Just because Satan is a smooth liar, don't give him more credit than he deserves. Sure, he can lie, but as a Believer he cannot control you. The Bible lays out God's plan for earth, so we get a sneak peak at the future. Christ defeated Satan's control of earth when He died on the cross and resurrected three days later. When Christ comes back Satan will be forever bound to Hell, unable to whisper lies again.

Whenever I catch myself taking inventory of my every flaw, or start in on some other ludicrous version of a "pep talk," I repeat verses to myself instead. I'm learning to distinguish Satan's lies from God's truth. And in case I'm feeling especially sucky or vulnerable, I know that Scripture is always true because it's always from God.

However, memorizing verses without understanding God's character didn't make much of a difference in my life. It was just another task on my list of things to do. Finding out I was a "New Creation" didn't mean much to me until I knew more about the Creator. The Bible was really just a bunch of words until I understood the Author's voice. Learning who God is—His character, His personality, His heart—infused meaning into every word on every page of the Bible. I could hear Him talking and, because I trusted His goodness, I was finally able to listen.

I am not the person I once was (not because I am trying harder) but because I learned how to fill in the following blank with truth instead of lies:

God is _____.

In the past, I filled in the blank with words like "judgmental," "suspicious," "mean," "arrogant" so it's no wonder I felt the way I did. Those were lies Satan wanted me to believe. I felt like a lost cause because I thought God was a harsh judge who enjoyed nothing more than striking His gavel on all of my mistakes. Condemning me. Judging me. Strike, strike, strike.

However, I was filling in the blanks incorrectly. Yes, God judges right from wrong, but the Old and New Testament paint God as the perfect balance of all-loving, all-knowing, and all-powerful. God is the Father, Son, and Holy Spirit. He made me, loves me, and fights *for* me not *against* me. When I learned how to fill in the blanks with this in mind, and fully believed it in my heart, I had hope. My world turned upside down.

Try filling in the blanks with the following words and see how your view of yourself changes as a result:

1. God is All-Loving.

I've searched for love in many places—some good, some bad. In the past, no matter how much love I tried to suck out of people and activities here on earth, I still felt empty at the end of the day. It's true that if we all have a God-shaped hole in our hearts, nothing but His love will fill the void.

People, even good people, are disappointing. Anthony loves me a lot, but even his love is not enough to complete me. It's just not. We have different needs, and I can't expect him to fulfill my every need, every moment of every day...although I still don't see why not sometimes.

The only lasting love is perfect love. And perfect love? It only comes from God. He sent His Son to die for me even though I am flawed. His love is unconditional and limitless:

For this is how God loved the world: He gave his one and only Son, so that everyone who believes in him will not perish but have eternal life. John 3:16

But God showed his great love for us by sending Christ to die for us while we were still sinners. Romans 5:8

2. God is All-Knowing.

Every night before my kids go to bed, I remind them that God has a special plan for them. They get giddy and excited, "What is it? What is it?" and I tell them we don't know yet but if we listen, God will give us clues. For my daughter, she loves drawing and making up stories and wants to be an author/illustrator. Who knows? Maybe that's what God has planned for her. My four-year-old little boy wants to grow up to be a construction worker and piano player—but hates manual labor and refuses to take music lessons ("Why would I?" he explains, "I'm already perfect at it!"). Maybe he has more to learn about his plan before he commits to anything.

God knows every detail of our futures before we are even born. The more we get to know Him the more closely we fulfill our dreams. Our respective futures are unique, designed especially for you and me. It's exciting to think the plans are set, are good, and that He gives us clues through our individual gifting and talents. He is all-knowing. We aren't, but He is.

As a little girl I would give speeches and narrate my day as if I were writing an autobiography. Despite these early clues, I let fear and insecurity prevent me from leaning in to God's plans and writing books and speaking to girls. However, God also knew that my experiences in college would fuel a passion for helping young women discover how truly valuable they are in Christ.

Even though it took me longer to figure out my plans, and I'm still learning the specifics, it is so fulfilling to use my God-given talents to help others. I'm finally trusting that God knows everything, and listening to His voice (through praying and reading His words in the Bible) is helping me live out my purpose. There is no problem He cannot answer.

Here are some verses to remind yourself that God is all-knowing and has a plan for you:

> *This was his eternal plan, which he carried out through Christ Jesus our Lord.* *Ephesians 3:11*

> *"For I know the plans I have for you," declares the Lord, "plans to prosper you and not to harm you, plans to give you hope and a future." Jeremiah 29:11 NIV*

> *The Lord Almighty has sworn, "Surely as I have planned so it will be, and as I have purposed, so it will happen." Isaiah 14:24*

*I love this one!!!! The words "eternal plan" are so comforting to me!! God is not wringing his hands worried over the future—the future of the world, or the future of me. His plans are eternal. In the end, Jesus will come back to right all wrongs. Good wins. The story is already written, and the ending for all those who believe is absolutely beautiful.

3. God is All-Powerful.

If you believe in Creation, then surely you respect the power of God. With a word, He spoke absolutely everything into existence. Everything—flowers, trees, people, frogs—everything. And all of creation is synchronized. Honeybees eat nectar from flowers to make honey, but they also spread pollen which affects the food supply of humans. It blows my mind. The majesty of it all is astounding. To me, mountains are more spectacular than oceans—but either way, impressive.

When I pray, I sometimes forget God's power—mostly because there are a couple aspects of my life where my faith is incredibly weak. I have prayed for years for a situation that secretly I believe will never change, because it never does. However, if God wants to change my situation, He certainly has the power to do so:

> *You faithfully answer our prayers with awesome deeds, O God our savior. You are the hope of everyone on earth, even those who sail on distant seas. You formed the mountains by your power and armed yourself with mighty strength.*
> *Psalms 65:6*

Ephesians 6:10 reminds us what to do with God's awesome power: Rest in it. Let His strength make you strong. It says, "Finally, be strong in the Lord and in his mighty power." For me, this is way more important than getting my way all the time. What would happen if God said yes to my every prayer request? One thing is for sure, I would be married to my seventh grade crush—so I'm glad the answer is sometimes no.

I can rely on God's power and not push through life by sheer grit and determination, thinking my way is always right. God created the world and broke the hold of sin and death through Jesus. Surely trusting in His power, and not my own, is best. Here are two of my favorite verses that demonstrate the power of God:

He gives power to the weak and strength to the powerless. Psalms 106:42

Now he is far above any ruler or authority or power or leader or anything else—not only in this world but also in the world to come. Ephesians 1:21

So, if there were a person that knew what was best for you, had the power to make it happen, and loved you immensely—wouldn't you trust that person?

With that being said, I was still confused about one more aspect of God...the Trinity. Besides being an excellent name for a Catholic high school, I didn't know what it meant.

THE TRINITY

Father + Son + Spirit = God

The Trinity refers to the Father, Son, and Holy Spirit under the umbrella (or Godhead) of God. So we have one God with three distinct personalities. Another way of saying it is one God, three persons. It's sort of like how even though I'm one person, I have different roles. Under the umbrella of "Katie" is "mom, wife, and daughter." All three words describe me, but individually they can't really stand alone. I'm not just a wife, I'm a mom. I'm not just a mom, I'm a daughter.

When I'm acting as a mom, different qualities come out (compassion, protectiveness, guidance). Similarly, when I'm acting as a wife and daughter, different qualities come out too (mainly in the form of complaining). I'm still compassionate as a wife, but in a different way than when I'm compassionate as a mom. Describing me as "just a mom" is not really accurate because even though I'm one person I have different roles.

Side note: even though I'm not just a mom, my kids don't seem to notice. The other day I overheard them bashing my new haircut…while I was driving them in the car! It ended with my son saying "it's bad but at least she can still wear it different ways." How generous. At least it beats the time my daughter eyeballed me up and down and observed "Some mommies are fat. Some are not. Don't worry, Mommy. You're not fat, just your butt is."

Even though my kids have never gotten the memo that I have other roles beyond serving them, the Trinity works the same way. God the Father, Son, and Holy Spirit are individual persons summed up in one ultimate person, God. You can't consider

God as just a Father, because the roles of the Son and Holy Spirit matter too. To understand God as a whole, let's look at each of the different persons of the Trinity a little closer:

1. God the Father

God the Father is reassuring to me because I had a good dad. However, not everyone has a good earthly father so to some I'm sure the concept of "God the Father" is not so appealing. One of the weirdest funerals I've ever been to was my husband's grandfather. He was not the best dad, and the nicest thing the eulogist could say was "this was a man of many regrets." It was either that or get plastered with tomatoes at the pulpit.

I will never forget that day. No one cried. And—I probably shouldn't admit this—but my husband actually bought a rental house during the funeral! He was texting with a realtor seconds before the poor eulogist tried to make the most out of an awkward situation. His grandfather's poor parenting and life choices led to a funeral that was, well, just another day.

Despite the legacy of his grandfather, my husband Anthony is a fantastic dad. Usually at night, Anthony and I chain-watch Netflix until we drag ourselves to bed. However, our little girl is currently obsessed with surprises and all things "special." Instead of vegging out on the couch after a long day's work, he took the time to draw a picture of her favorite cartoon character (Twilight Sparkle from *My Little Pony*) and write a sweet note for her to find in her lunch box the next day. Gestures like that remind Rylie that her daddy loves her, delights in her, and finds *her* special.

While Anthony adores Rylie, his love pales in comparison to how God the Father feels about you. The Bible describes God as "Abba, Father" which, when translated, means "Daddy:"

> *And because we are his children, God has sent the Spirit of his Son into our hearts, prompting us to call out, "Abba, Father." Galatians 4:6*

If God were to leave a note in your lunchbox, this is what it would say:

> *But those who trust in the LORD WILL FIND NEW STRENGTH. They will soar high on wings like eagles. They will run and not grow weary. They will walk and not faint. Isaiah 40:31*

2. God the Son

In a Sunday school class full of six year olds, the teacher asks, "What is small, brown with a furry tail, and eats nuts in your backyard?" A little boy shoots up his hand and says, "Well, it *sounds* like a squirrel, but I'm going to go with Jesus."

Down here in the Bible Belt, we hear the name of Jesus often. So often, that sometimes we tune out when we hear His name or answer "Jesus" because we feel like we're supposed to. Answering this way is not only socially acceptable, it's almost expected. Makes us look good. But when push comes to shove, what is Jesus really like? Is He the answer to every question?

God the Father makes me feel secure. His big strong daddy arms are reliable, loving, and trustworthy. Jesus, on the other hand, makes me feel like I can conquer the world. In fact, in John 16:33 Jesus says, " I have told you all this so that you may have peace in me. Here on earth you will have many trials and sorrows. But take heart, because I have overcome the world." Isn't that awesome? I love it because Jesus is so realistic. He knows this world has trouble and doesn't sugar-coat anything. But I also love how He speaks with such confidence and authority. He defeated evil once and for all and through Him everything can be okay.

Colossians 1:15-16a explains Jesus this way, "Christ is the visible image of the invisible God. He existed before anything was created and is supreme over all creation, for through him God created everything in the heavenly realms and on earth." In other words, Jesus is God and existed before earth was even formed. Colossians goes on to say in verses 19 & 20, "For God in all his fullness was pleased to live in Christ, and through him God reconciled everything to himself. He made peace with everything in heaven and on earth by means of Christ's blood on the cross."

Jesus was and is fully God and fully man. He fulfilled the promise God gave in the very beginning of the Bible that He would bless all nations through Abraham. When Christ returns, all wrongs will be made right and peace and perfection will again rule. Between you and me, I can't wait.

3. God the Holy Spirit

As a little kid I was convinced there was a gremlin science lab under my bed (you know from the 1980s horror franchise *Gremlins*. I saw a preview on TV and was never the same). If the sheet wasn't pulled over my mouth at night, one of the gremlins would steal my lips and look at them under a microscope. Despite sweating my guts out on a nightly basis, I maintained the mountain of sheets and blankets on my head. But here is the worst part: when I first heard about the Holy Ghost, I was secretly afraid of Him too.

However, I was wrong to lump the person of the Holy Ghost in with ghost stories and horror movies...although that doesn't stop me from preferring the word "spirit" to "ghost." The unknown in the spiritual realm might give me pause, but knowing the Holy Spirit reassures me. I don't have to check under my bed anymore.

One of my huge misconceptions about the Holy Spirit was figuring out the right pronoun. Was the Holy Spirit a "he" or an "it?" Because the Trinity is three persons in one, each of the persons—Father, Son, and Holy Spirit—can stand alone. In other words, the Holy Spirit is a "who" and can be referred to as a "he" just like we refer to the other parts of the Trinity, God and Jesus, as "he."

The Holy Spirit is who came to represent the physical presence of Jesus after He died, resurrected, and returned to Heaven. Jesus disciples were distraught when He told them that He was going to physically leave them. However, in John 14:16-17 Jesus assures them "And I will ask the Father, and he will give you another Advocate, who will never leave you. He is the Holy Spirit, who leads into all truth. The world cannot receive him, because it isn't looking for him and doesn't recognize him. But you know him, because he lives with you now and later will be in you."

In other words, the power of Jesus—who could perform miracles and had a perfect relationship with God the Father—lives in me because the Holy Spirit lives in me. The disciples had to rely on the physical form of Jesus for guidance, but God sent the Holy Spirit to be a spiritual guide, or Advocate, to live in the hearts of believers.

The more I learn about the person of the Holy Spirit, the more my eyes are opened to the amazing power living inside me. For example, on my own my nature sucks. I'm afraid of everything from violent home invasions to gross public bathrooms. I'm bossy. I'm arrogant. I'm insecure. I contradict myself. However, because the Holy Spirit lives inside me, I have access 24-7 to the same power and perfection of Jesus Christ.

Jesus might not be physically walking around in a pair of sandals anymore, but His same power sure is. Thank goodness I am not bound by my own selfish nature because Matthew 19:26 says "with God all things are possible." Instead of relying on my own limited power, I can rely on God's power in me. After all, according to Ephesians 5:9 "this light within you produces what is good and right and true."

Even though I'm still selfish, there's now a light in me that produces good fruit. Galatians 6:22-23 says "But the fruit of the Spirit is love, joy, peace, patience, kindness, goodness, faithfulness, gentleness and self-control." I have access to all this "fruit" because the more I know who the Holy Spirit is, the better I understand that His power and how His good qualities can supersede my bad ones. **"Spiritual fruit" is not a list of behaviors I have to force, instead it's a quality of life that naturally grows from my relationship with the Holy Spirit.**

The Holy Spirit helped me in a practical way just recently. Someone I've known for years hurt my feelings—like really, really, really hurt my feelings. It sucked. I was a hot mess over the situation for about a month until I finally decided to take some of my own advice and turn to God for help. This all happened as I was thinking and writing about the Holy Spirit, so

I finally just asked the Holy Spirit Himself to speak to me about my confrontation with my friend. And guess what?

It worked.

Some of my favorite verses came to mind and had a whole new meaning. Some strong Christian friends gave me some advice very consistent with those very same verses, and I thought— huh—so that's what it means to be "filled with the Spirit." You submit, ask, and listen. He brings to mind verses (which are after all divinely inspired) and uses other Christian people, circumstances, or thoughts consistent with the Scripture to send you a message. And I mean literally send you a message, not some abstract hocus-pocus concept, but an actual verse or spoken word. It's awesome. Peace replaced my stomach cramps.

Seeing God accurately will change how you fill in the blanks in your own life. Cross out misconceptions of God and you can cross out misconceptions of yourself:

God is ~~The Cruel Judge, An Aloof Observer, A Demanding Boss~~, Good.

I am ~~The Life of the Party, Girlfriend, Perfectionist~~, A New Creation.

Genesis 1:27 & 31 says "So God created human beings in his own image" and "Then God looked over all he had made, and he saw that it was very good!" You are created in God's image. It matters that He is good because He made you in His image. Through Him you have access to an Authentic Identity, and that identity is good.

If our Authentic Identity is what He thinks of us, and now we know how He thinks based on who He is—the question remains:

What does it mean to be a New Creation?

AUTHENTIC ID

A New Creation

Living as a New Creation requires a change of heart, not a personality transplant. Just because your sins are washed clean and you get a second chance at life doesn't mean you will be a bland robotic version of your former self. Your new forgiveness and identity does not give you license to do every depraved thing in the book and get away with it without consequence either. Again, a life of faith is about balance.

The balance is that, yes, God loves you and forgives you and sees you as full of potential—but He also expects you to honor Him through your heart and actions as well. I screw up on a regular basis, and I'm forgiven on a regular basis. What I've learned is that the more I know the character of God the more I want to please Him. He loves me so much that I can't help loving Him in return. Being a New Creation means my desire to please myself is replaced with a desire to please God which is ultimately way more satisfying and way, way (way, way, way) more fulfilling.

With that said, the Bible uses many different analogies to describe how God sees us, our Authentic Identities. I mentioned that one of my favorites is God is the potter, I am the clay. Isaiah 64:8 says, "And yet, O LORD, you are our Father. We are the clay, and you are the potter. We all are formed by your hand." I like thinking of myself this way because it means God is in control; if I break, He can fix me. Even better, any brokenness in me is really an opportunity for light to shine through. God molds me into a beautiful masterpiece and all I have to do is allow Him to pick up the pieces I've lost along the way.

However, the three analogies that meant the most to me in my early twenties were **Daughter, Friend, and Bride.** All three analogies represent deepening layers of intimacy. For example, when I finally submitted fully to God I related to being His Daughter more than anything. He was the authority figure, the Father figure, and I was His child. He guided me, gave me advice. The more comfortable I felt in His presence, the more I could relate to Him as a Friend as well. I could be myself around Him and not tip-toe around issues I was afraid to bring up to my Father. Eventually—and this one took some getting used to—I began to see myself as a Bride and God as the elated Groom. Not in a sexual way. Gross. No, God calls me into a relationship with Him that shares that same intimate closeness that Anthony and I share. Spouses can speak volumes with just a glance of the eye. There is an intimacy to marriage to which no other relationship can compare. That's how I feel with God. He *knows* me. And I know Him.

No matter my confusion, no matter my scars, no matter how I feel on any certain day God sees me as His Daughter, His friend, His Bride. I have to remind myself that the old me is gone. This is who I am now:

As a New Creation, I am God's:

1. DAUGHTER.

And I will be your Father, and you will be my sons and Daughters, says the LORD Almighty. 2 Corinthians 6:18

2. FRIEND.

Now you are my friends, since I have told you everything the Father told me. John 15:15b

3. BRIDE.

For your Creator will be your husband; the LORD of Heaven's Armies is his name! He is your Redeemer, the Holy One of Israel, the God of all the earth. Isaiah 54:5

The best part of finding out who you really are is there is no pressure to be a Daughter, Friend, or Bride. **You don't *try to be* a New Creation, you just *are* a New Creation**. And the freedom of *being* instead of *doing* applies to your motivation for following God as well. Your motivation for obeying God, and claiming your identity, doesn't have to be fear or guilt—just like there's no reason to guilt or scare yourself into being more of a New Creation. After all, 1 John 4:19 says "We love each other because he loved us first."

The more you learn about who God is and His love for you, the more you will want to know Him and your motivation for everything you do will come from a place of security and love.

Authentic ID #1

Daughter

The definition of your identity as a God's Daughter is this: you are God's child, the daughter of a King, heir to the kingdom of God. When God calls me a child of God, He is referring to my identity and describing the way He sees me. He is the loving Father; I am the beloved Daughter. God values me because I am His.

Here is what Grace Ann had to say about being God's Daughter:

The more I tried to establish my identity in partying, the more I lost myself. I was getting farther away from becoming my own person and I got stuck in a downward spiral of emptiness. The core of who I was became empty. When my identity was based on fun, it was unstable, weak, and hollow.

When I finally fully accepted Christ, I was able to establish my identity as His beloved Daughter! Life as a Daughter is bright, joyful, and beautiful. When God is your center, there is a level of peace that can't be found in anything else. I was suffocating in a life of partying, but once I accepted Christ as my Savior I could finally breathe! I realized I'm a Daughter of the one true King, and I finally understood how deeply and unconditionally He loves every single thing about me...Knowing God has allowed me to live life to the fullest.

I have such a soft spot in my heart for Grace Ann. She reminds me of myself—well—she reminds me of who I *wanted* to be in college. Her transformation is amazing, and her core is not hollow anymore.

While Grace Ann embraces God as her Father, if you had a bad dad, the concept of "God the Father" may turn you off completely. My friend Elizabeth had a hard time separating the actions of her earthly father from the overwhelming love of her heavenly Father. Because she feared the man who raised her, she was suspicious of God too. She couldn't reconcile the two in her mind:

...Later on, as a teenager, because I grew up in an environment where not only myself but my mother was beaten also, I developed an intense hatred of my dad. The real effect of my anger though was that it was turned inward on myself. I felt ugly and rejected because the one person who should have treated me kindly and taught me how beautiful I was did nothing but abuse and neglect me instead. Maybe the worst part was that deep in my heart I was still longing for his love and affection—and I was still longing to love him also.

I had always known that God was real but naturally, because of my home life, I couldn't understand Him as a loving Father. Because I felt so betrayed by my own father, I started to act out in all of the ways that a hurting teenager normally does—maybe to get my dad's attention, but maybe to get God's also. But the emptiness and the pain never got better, only worse. I couldn't see any reason for living and felt like I had no purpose—that I was good for nothing. I hated myself so much that I shut out every possibility of believing that life could be better.

God is the PERFECT Father who loves and accepts you, protects you, guides you, and sacrifices for you. Unlike some earthly fathers, He can be trusted. After years of searching, here is what my friend learned about the character of God the Father:

I decided to go to Bible school—to search for God, but also to get away from my dad. While there, the Lord began to rescue my heart. It was during that season that Jesus somehow awakened me to His desire and longing for me to receive Him and His love. I was blown away to realize that God loved me for me. Not a better version of me, but the me that I was right then. I couldn't help but become transformed by that kind of love...

My prayer for all of us is that we realize how much we really ache for the touch of the Lord in our lives. No matter how good or bad our lives have been, God created within each of us a longing that can only be satisfied by Him. May Jesus awaken our hearts to the beauty of who He is and the love that He makes available.

Unlike an unreliable earthly father, John 14:18 offers us a promise, "No, I will not abandon you as orphans—I will come to you." When Jesus went to Heaven, the Holy Spirit came to live in our hearts as a constant reminder of God's love. We are never alone. God the Father will not abandon you. Ever. And He will love "you for you" just as Elizabeth discovered He loved "me for me."

But it gets even better. If God is the King of kings and you are His Daughter, then guess what? When you place your trust in Christ, you are a princess! Woo hoo! This works for me because

I act like a princess half the time anyway (case in point: I've been married almost 10 years and have never ever mowed our lawn… *and I never will*.)

Like any child of a King, you also are heir to an inheritance. You are a certifiable trust fund baby! Unlike a trust fund with stipulations on your age, marital status, or college major you can claim your inheritance in Christ right away. Ephesians 1:5-11 does a great job of breaking down your identity as a child of God. According to the passage, you are:

1. ADOPTED. You are adopted into God's family.

God decided in advance to adopt us into his own family by bringing us to Himself through Jesus Christ.

2. DELIGHTFUL. God delights in you.

This is what he wanted to do, and it gave him great pleasure. So we praise God for the glorious grace he has poured out on us who belong to his dear Son. He is so rich in kindness and grace that he purchased our freedom with the blood of his Son and forgave our sins. He has showered his kindness on us, along with all wisdom and understanding.

3. TRUSTWORTHY. God reveals His plan to you.

God has now revealed to us his mysterious plan regarding Christ, a plan to fulfill his own good pleasure. And this is the plan: At the right time he will bring everything together under the authority of Christ—everything in heaven and on earth.

4. RICH. As a child of God, you receive an inheritance.

Furthermore, because we are united with Christ, we have received an inheritance from God, for he chose us in advance, and he makes everything work out according to his plan.

Clearly, you are an heir and beloved Daughter, but your inheritance is even more beautiful and encouraging: access to all of the qualities of Jesus Christ. We don't have to be perfect to gain acceptance as God's children; we just have to believe He sent his son Jesus to die for us. When Jesus rose three days after His crucifixion, He defeated evil and we now have access to the same power that raised Him from the dead, which is our inheritance as Daughters of the King.

If our Authentic Identity is a Daughter of God, what else does that entail? Our inheritance is powerful, yes. But more specifically, as Daughters of God we are:

☑ **Forgiven.** God forgives His Daughters.

☑ **Courageous.** God tells His girls to stand strong. To not be afraid (365 times in the Bible actually).

☑ **Restored.** When we return to our Father He restores us to our position as princess no matter where we've been.

Forgiven

A sorority sister once asked me if I found my boyfriends in the unemployment line. Because she was hilarious, and because she was sort of right, I forgave her. However, after a bad string of relationships in college it was much harder to forgive myself. In fact, I thought if I felt bad enough about my imperfect choices I could punish myself back into God's good graces. Wrong! According to Psalm 103:12, "He has removed our sins as far from us as the east is from the west." **My Heavenly Father forgives me, so I am forgiven.**

There's a difference between being forgiven and feeling forgiven. I had a really hard time with that. Intellectually, I knew that Jesus nailed my sin to the cross and His death and resurrection made me clean. However, certain cues—songs, smells, names—would remind me of bad memories and I would feel ashamed. Even though my sin was removed and God forgave me I still felt haunted by my past. Because your past will always be there, my best advice is to deal with it. You are forgiven by God, but you can't rely on feeling forgiven to remind you of your new freedom.

For me, I had to fill my mind with constant reminders of my identity as a forgiven person. When I didn't feel forgiven, I would remind myself of certain verses. Instead of reliving a vivid memory when a certain song came on the radio, I would say "thank you God for forgiving me," and then I would read Psalm 103. Salve to my wounded heart. If your heart feels raw when a particularly awful memory flashes through your mind, try having your own go-to verse to remind yourself that you are forgiven. The sting of bad memories can and does fade when you replace the devil's lie with God's truth of forgiveness.

If a Bible passage is long, I usually skip over it. However, please bear with me because there is something special, life-changing even, about Psalm 103. Here is an excerpt but please read the rest on your own. www.bible.com has a free Bible app if you need one:

> *...Let all that I am praise the lord; may I never forget the good things he does for me... He fills my life with good things... He does not punish us for all our sins; he does not deal harshly with us, as we deserve. For his unfailing love toward those who fear him is as great as the height of the heavens above the earth.* **He has removed our sins as far from us as the east is from the west. The lord is like a father to His children, tender and compassionate to those who fear him.** *Excerpts from Psalm 103*

See yourself through God's eyes. When you put your faith in Christ, you assume the qualities of Christ. You are a new person filled with the same power that gave Jesus His power when He was on earth.

When Anthony and I were dating—wow, our relationship was different than my others—he gave me a bookmark that had a chart on it. On one side of the chart were lies and the other truth of how God felt about me. I didn't really understand all the words on the chart because it was written in churchy (annoying) language, so I made my own chart of what helped me the most and put it on the very last page of the book.

Every time I didn't feel forgiven, I whipped out my bookmark and read some verses that reminded me of my identity as a Daughter of God. While my chart is not exactly bookmark-sized, I included two so you can rip one out and put it somewhere easily accessible—a bathroom mirror, the car, a journal—at least until you memorize the verses that mean the most to you.

Reminding yourself of your identity as a forgiven Daughter of God is a battle you don't have to fight alone. God will help you, but memorizing Scripture is like putting on armor to deflect the lies of Satan. For me, I believed so many lies I needed to build up an arsenal of verses. I recommend being prepared for attack:

> *Therefore, put on every piece of God's armor so you will be able to resist the enemy in the time of evil. Then after the battle you will still be standing firm. Stand your ground, putting on the belt of truth and the body armor of God's righteousness. For shoes, put on the peace that comes from the Good News so that you will be fully prepared. In addition to all of these, hold up the shield of faith to stop the fiery arrows of the devil. Put on salvation as your helmet, and take the sword of the Spirit, which is the word of God. Ephesians 6:13-17*

COURAGEOUS

One time in a job interview, the owner of a company asked me to name my biggest fear. I replied, "I used to be afraid of big dogs—*dramatic pause*—so I got one." Ugh. That's so not true. On a whim I woke up one day and decided to get a yellow lab and name him Frank. There was no rhyme or reason. That beautiful dog was my best friend...until I met Anthony like 6 months later. Frank was the only vicious yellow lab in history and after he tried to kill Anthony the ten-thousandth time he lived the rest of his life with my parents. Poor Mom and Dad. In reality, 10 billion other things rank higher than dogs on My List of Worst Fears Ever.

One of my most recent paralyzing fears had to do with starting www.laneofroses.com. I was so afraid to fail, so afraid of not being good enough, so afraid of what people might think that it took me ten years to go for it. Ten years.

In the back of my mind, I always knew I wanted to speak and write to a college audience. But I figured someone else, *anyone else*, could do a better job. I was panicked about expressing my beliefs—not all of my ideas are great and sometimes I'm hard to understand. But so what? I will make mistakes, but letting fear (both of the known and the unknown) dictate my actions is no way to live.

Last year, Anthony wanted me to meet his friend Jeff who runs a prayer ministry in town. Truth be told, I'd always been a little suspicious of "prayer ministries." Probably because I went to an especially charismatic high school church meeting once and when my friend and I tried to leave a huge man blocked the door and wouldn't let us. It was scary—I swear I have PTSD from that experience. However, Anthony assured me the last thing Jeff would ever do is freak anyone out and invited me to meet up with him and pray.

Still, no thanks.

After a few rebuffed invitations, Anthony decided to try one more time. Now, if you know me well, you know that I fix my hair one of two styles: a crazy, frizzy ponytail to exercise class or blow-dried with 40 products for regular, everyday life. I do this not out of vanity, but out of concern for others of course. Left unchecked, I have mad scientist hair—a shocking mix of wiry curls and stick straight hair with cowlicks in all the wrong places. Here's the miracle: the morning I finally met up with Anthony and Jeff to pray at Panera (*in public*, oh no!) I had the crazy, frizzy ponytail. Clearly, I was not planning on going at all.

When we got there, Anthony and Jeff talked and I was pretty quiet at first. However, Jeff is a really respected photographer in town. His pictures are the backdrop for the evening news and are plastered everywhere in the Lexington airport. I love artistic people more than anything, so it was fun—not awkward or contrived. He didn't block the exit or anything.

Before I knew it I was telling Jeff about my idea for Lane of Roses. I admitted my fears that I wouldn't be good enough to run it, and he asked if he could pray for me. In the restaurant. In front of everybody. Strangely, I wanted him to. When he prayed I felt released. He prayed about how God sees me as His Daughter—created to run free in a field of possibility—not shrink in fear. My worst fears didn't seem so bad. In fact, they suddenly felt very, very small.

I'm not made to be a slave to fear. You were not made to be a slave to fear. We don't have to be afraid of anything. But even if we are, we don't have to bow to fear. Ever. Courage is not an absence of fear, it's moving forward in spite of it.

As Daughters of a powerful King, we were made to step out in faith. To go for it. That's living in freedom, not shrinking from fear but rising above it. Opportunities to be afraid will never go away, but like any temptation, fear is not a sin unless we act on it or give in to it.

Jeff was made to take beautiful pictures and pray for people. Anthony was made to strategize, dream, and create systems to benefit businesses and organizations (and marry me—score!). I was made to write this book—eek, regardless of whether anyone but my mom reads it—manage the Lane of Roses site, raise my sweet kids, and have coffee with girls. Fear doesn't have to hold you back. That's real courage.

There's a special plan for your life too as a cherished Daughter of God. After all, Romans 12:6 says, "In His grace, God has given us different gifts for doing certain things well." Don't let fear hold you back from finding out how to boldly live out the plan for your life. Odds are, whatever that plan is you will absolutely love it. Don't waste time being scared. You are a princess with special gifts, so go for it.

Here's a good verse to remind you of your identity—hardwired with courage:

> *Such love has no fear, because perfect love expels all fear.*
> *If we are afraid, it is for fear of punishment, and this*
> *shows that we have not fully experienced his perfect love.*
> *1 John 4:17-19*

P.S. This has nothing to do with the price of eggs, but Anthony said I'm making him seem too good to be true and he's getting annoyed with himself. He said if he were reading this as someone else he would want to either puke or punch us both in the face. Sorry for making him seem perfect. Trust me, he's not...he's stubborn to a fault (a fault!) and almost as selfish as I am sometimes.

RESTORED

Check out Luke 15 to read the parable of the Lost Son in full, but here's a recap. A rebellious son, the prodigal, wants his inheritance right away. The father gives it to him, but the son squanders it in no time flat. A famine strikes and the son is forced to get a job feeding pigs. He's so hungry he longs to eat the food the pigs eat when it hits him: his father's servants at least get fed well.

Because he feels unworthy to return as a son, he decides to beg his dad to at least be a hired hand. However, when his father sees him coming he embraces him, puts a ring on his finger and throws a huge party in honor of his son's return before the son gets the chance to deliver his rehearsed plea.

While the father is ecstatic, the prodigal's older brother is furious and bitter. The brother follows every rule and complains that he never gets so much as a goat for his obedience; his brother, on the other hand, squanders his share of the family fortune on prostitutes and wild living and gets a fattened calf? No fair.

The father answers the older brother that everything he has is his, but he should come celebrate because his sibling was lost but now he is found. He was dead, now he's alive.

The parable of The Lost Son is the perfect example of how your identity as a child of God works because it provides a script of what the Father says to us whether we are feeling unworthy or bitter. The prodigal son was a rebellious wild child who later felt worthless; the brother followed the rules and felt self-righteous and resentful. I know I relate to feeling like both of the brothers.

If you are more of a prodigal wild child or simply struggle with feelings of worthiness, Luke 15 gives some direct quotes of what the Father says to you:

> **Prodigal:** *"I am no longer worthy of being called your son. Please take me on as a hired servant."*
>
> **Father:** *And while he was still a long way off, his father saw him coming. Filled with love and compassion, he ran to his son, embraced him, and kissed him.*
>
> *"We must celebrate with a feast, for this son of mine was dead and has now returned to life. He was lost, but now he is found." So the party began.*

The prodigal felt unworthy because of the mistakes he had made. But did the father disown him? Agree he was disgusting? No way! The father *ran* to his son, *embraced* him, and *kissed* him. No matter how dirty you feel—and trust me while I never envied the food of any pigs, I certainly dated my fair share—God welcomes you back to him with open arms.

That's what it means to be redeemed, or restored. **As God's Daughter you are not just accepted, you are restored to how God intended you to be.** Psalm 103:4 says God "redeemed my life from the pit and crowned me with love and compassion." When you come home to God, you are redeemed by faith to your rightful place as princess; you are the Daughter of the one true King.

Remember when I thought God would look at me with disgust in the background of my worst memory? Instead I pictured him embracing me. This story confirms the truth that God treats us, not as our sins deserve, but with mercy and love. So if you are hoping beyond hope that God will shrug and say "I guess so" when you beg to come home—you're wrong. He'll throw a royal robe around your shoulders and celebrate. Like it's 1999.

God may not judge me as my sins deserve, but I am certainly guilty of being judgmental and/or bitter myself. So for the times you can relate more to the rule-following brother—or are resentful because you feel like you're being screwed over—look at what the Father says to you:

> **Rule Following Brother:** *"All these years I've slaved for you and never once refused to do a single thing you told me to... Yet when this son of yours comes back after squandering your money on prostitutes, you celebrate by killing the fattened calf!"*

> **Father:** *"Look, dear son, you have always stayed by me, and everything I have is yours. We had to celebrate this happy day. For your brother was dead and has come back to life! He was lost, but now he is found!"*

The brother in the story felt like his excellent rule-following behavior made him worthier of his father's attention. He was insulted that he didn't get more rewarded than his wayward sibling. However, when the brother refused to attend the prodigal's welcome home party he was in for some shocking news. The father begs him to join the party, but it's clear the playing field is level. Everything the father has already belongs to the brother, so he doesn't offer him more. The brother already has it all.

Being great at following rules does not make the brother any worthier than his prodigal sibling. What makes him worthy is his identity as a son. Both sons are invited to the party because they are both just that—sons. Their behavior is very different, but their identities are the same.

If you are feeling unworthy, you are not. You are a beloved Daughter of God; He runs to you and celebrates your homecoming no matter where you've been. If you are feeling bitter, you can let it go. Everything God has is yours. You are His Daughter too and He *begs* you to join the party. You are wanted.

As Daughters of God, we are invited to cast everything on Him—worries, fears, insecurities, feelings of unworthiness and resentment, bitterness—everything. That's just a benefit of your Authentic Identity:

> *Come to me, all of you who are weary and carry heavy burdens, and I will give you rest. Take my yoke upon you. Let me teach you, because I am humble and gentle at heart, and you will find rest for your souls. For my yoke is easy and the burden I give you is light. Matthew 11:28-30*

Whether your burden is feeling unworthy or bitter, God can give you rest. You are His Daughter by faith, not feeling. He forgives you, so you are forgiven. He redeems you, so you are redeemed. You can have courage because your Heavenly Father loves you and gives you access to an inheritance that is bigger than you can ask or imagine just because you are His child.

Authentic ID #2

Friend

When God calls us Friends, He's inviting us to share with Him in a way we would share with a friend. Even though my dad is great, we have never stayed up until 2am gabbing about boy problems. With friends we can vent, we can laugh, we can cry, we can have fun. Basically, we can be honest, *really* honest—like if you have to go pee and you're on the phone you still go pee—honest.

When I asked Melody what it meant to have God as her very best Friend, she said very simply:

> *Knowing that God calls me His Friend helps me to not look at Him as some distant mythological creature but rather someone that enjoys being with me. Cares for me. Is here present on Earth with me. And as enjoyable as my most fun friends!*

Last year when my daughter was in preschool she made her first best friend, Emma. Rylie and Emma were inseparable. They connected in a way that not even their teachers could understand. The two of them spent every millisecond together and ignored the other kids on the playground. However, when preschool ended, Emma and her family moved several states away. Rylie was crestfallen, and even after a year she still talks about her best friend. In fact, she recently wrote her a note:

Emma,

You will always be my best friend forever. How is Kansas City?

I wish you could move back to Lexington.

But you can't.

Rylie

The sad truth is that sometimes even best friends go away. I know I've had friendships I swore would never end, but eventually fizzled out due to distance or personal change. I remember eating a Blizzard with my high school best friends during senior year—something we did a lot—thinking no matter what we would always be close. But I moved away. I visited for a few years, but after a while we drifted apart. While that pains a sentimental fool like me, there is a relationship that never has to end—a relationship so close it defines me. I am a Friend of God:

So now we can rejoice in our wonderful new relationship with God because our Lord Jesus Christ has made us Friends of God. Romans 5:11

Jesus Christ is the perfect Friend. In fact, He proved it—He *died* for us. John 15:13 says "there is no greater love than to lay down one's life for one's friends." Jesus is the Friend you can confide in, the Friend you can trust. He doesn't gossip about you behind your back, convince you to buy the dress that makes your butt look ten times bigger, or secretly wish you would screw up just so He can feel better about Himself. He is good and true, and you are worthy of His friendship by simply admitting you want it. That's all.

You don't have to look prettier or be more popular to be worthy of His friendship; all He asks is you give yourself, your whole self, as a friend in return. A real friendship requires mutual communication and affection. We communicate with God through prayer and reading what He has to say in the Bible. When I hear that little voice in my head, I listen closely. If the voice I hear is consistent with Scripture, it's God. He talks to me and I just need to be still enough to listen:

Be still, and know that I am God! Psalm 46:10a

As a New Creation you are also a Friend of God. And Friends of God are:

☑ **Accepted.** God accepts His friends despite any imperfections.

☑ **Great Hostesses.** God lives in us and all we have to do as His friends is invite Him in and be aware of His presence.

☑ **Capable of Amazing Things.** When Jesus walked on water, so did His friend Peter. With God as our friend, all things are possible.

ACCEPTED

Recently, Isaiah 41:8 stopped me in my tracks. It's ones of those verses that's easy to pass over—"But as for you, Israel my servant, Jacob my chosen one; descended from Abraham my friend..."—but the word "friend" made me think. If God literally called Abraham "my friend," what did Abraham do to earn that friendship? Was it perfect behavior? Nope. It was faith.

It should relieve you to know that behavior-wise, Abraham could be a real dirt bag. He would take huge leaps of faith, but then do something totally stupid out of fear. Once, a king noticed his beautiful wife Sarah and Abraham pretended to be her brother so the king could sleep with her without having to kill her husband first. Gross. That makes me so mad. If a king wanted to sleep with me, Anthony had better not go down without a fight.

However, in Genesis 22 Abraham was also willing to sacrifice his son—his promised son, his only shot at fulfilling the promise God gave to him—just because God asked. Abraham may not have had perfect (or even consistent) behavior but his faith was huge.

The same is true for us. In my life, I've made some dirt bag decisions too, yet I am still a Friend of God. My identity as a Friend of God doesn't change because I screw up or lose sight of what's important. One of my favorite passages is Mark 9:22-24:

> ... A father begs Jesus to heal his son from demon possession and says, "Have mercy on us and help us, if you can."

> "What do you mean, 'If I can?' Jesus asked. "Anything is possible if a person believes."

The father instantly cried out, "I do believe, but help me overcome my unbelief!"

If that's not me, I don't know what is. I love the father in this passage because I have to pray the same thing. It's normal to have doubts, but that doesn't mean your doubts are valid. Jesus cast out the evil spirit out of the little boy, and His ability to do so didn't depend on whether or not the father thought it was possible. And Abraham knew that about God—that his human feelings didn't impact the power and authority of an almighty God.

True, Abraham may have freaked out and made some mistakes out of doubt and fear. But when push came to shove Abraham left his home country because God said so and was willing to sacrifice his son. He had faith. James 2:23 says "Abraham believed God, and God counted him as righteous because of his faith."

What's interesting is that what God thinks of Abraham— "God counted him as righteous because of his faith"—may not be how Abraham saw himself. Sure, he left his country and all, but he also lied about being Sarah's brother and slept with her maid when God's promise of a son was taking a little too long. I would be willing to bet that Abraham would recount his story differently. God recalls his faith, but if you asked Abraham I bet he would have an easier time recalling his failures.

But it doesn't matter ultimately how Abraham saw himself, or how you see yourself, because God sees us differently than we see ourselves. God accepts His friends. Romans 15:7 says, "Accept one another, then, just as Christ accepted you, in order to bring praise to God." If God accepted Abraham because of his faith—his *imperfect* faith—He will accept you too.

If you believe in Christ and put your hope in Him you are accepted. Knowing I am accepted, not constantly trying to earn acceptance, frees me. I don't feel like I'm carrying an 800 pound gorilla on my back or have to look over my shoulder all the time trying to be good enough to be God's Friend. I am God's Friend. I am accepted—and although it shocks me—God is even pleased with me.

That is an identity I can live with.

And because I can't help it, here are a few verses on friendship. If this is how God sees you as a Friend, it makes sense to look for friends with these qualities too. After all, Jon Weece of Southland Christian Church says "Show me your friends, and I'll show you your future." With God as my Friend, my future just got a whole lot brighter:

As iron sharpens iron, so a friend sharpens a friend. Proverbs 27:17

There are "friends" who destroy each other, but a real friend sticks closer than a brother. Proverbs 18:24

The heartfelt counsel of a friend is as sweet as perfume and incense. Proverbs 27:6

GREAT HOSTESSES

Sometimes I'm a great hostess, and sometimes I'm...not. When we first got married, I mutated into an evil psycho before anyone came over because I wanted my house to be gorgeous and my food delicious. Or else. The last straw was when we hosted a group of students in our new house (new to us, it was built in the 1920s) and I furiously scrubbed floors while Anthony relaxed. I flew into a rage, screamed at my deer-in-the-headlights husband for not being stressed out enough, and acted like a martyr to prove how right I was. When the doorbell rang, however, I plastered an insta-smile on my face and laughed and joked with our guests while Anthony did not say a word the whole time. Oops.

That was an ah-ha moment for me, and I decided to let the perfect house, perfect hostess obsession go. I'm so glad I did! I've had so much more fun with family and friends. In the past, I would never have been able to have neighbors over on a whim. My friend Hannah and her kids came over for dinner one night spur of the moment and there were so many toys on the ground you couldn't tell if we had carpet or hardwood floors. The food was pretty rotten, but we had a blast. No one cared. And if they did, the best part is, I didn't care.

Of course, there is a balance. If I had invited Hannah over weeks in advance to celebrate her birthday, I would've picked up the toys and made something special for dinner. But on the fly, last minute, who cares? A real friend is a welcoming hostess no matter what.

Recently, my husband and I decided to do a Bible study together on being a great host. My husband's superpower is his ability to summarize. He reads some uber intellectual book on Christianity then gives me the bullet points. It's a wonderful system. I'm very well-read if you count hearing the summaries second-hand. If a book is particularly good, however, I will jump on board.

The latest and greatest Anthony book is *Hosting the Presence of God* by Bill Johnson. Anthony is reading the book and we're each filling out the workbook on our own. I love reading the Bible. I didn't use to, but now it seems so alive I can't get enough. But I also enjoy hearing what others have learned, and Bill's perspective is great. He says once we enter into relationship with God through faith in Jesus Christ, the Holy Spirit comes to live inside of us making us hosts of the presence of God.

Here is how Bill describes our role as a host:

If you were renting a house from me, I wouldn't walk into the home without an invitation, or at least without your permission. Though the house belongs to me and I am renting it to you, I am not going to barge in, ruffle through the refrigerator, and start cooking a meal for myself. Why? Although it is legally my house, it is under your charge and stewardship.

The Holy Spirit indwells every believer. The question is, how many believers are actually stewarding His Presence well?

Works and greater works, miracles and extraordinary miracles- these are the expression of a lifestyle that hosts God's Presence. Our job? Treat the One who possesses our lives as the honored Guest.

(Hosting the Presence of God Workbook pg 10)

My dad does a great job of hosting the presence of God, letting God enhance his gifts for the benefit of others...although he's not without flaw either. When it comes to communication over the phone, my dad is the world's worst responder. No matter what any of us text him—*What time is Thanksgiving dinner? When are you visiting? What's your favorite color?*—he always texts back "yes" and that's it. Clearly attention to detail is not one of his gifts, but Dad thankfully has others that make up for it.

Here is the verse my dad applies (well, tries to apply) daily:

Trust in the Lord with all your heart and lean not on your own understanding; in all your ways submit to him, and he will make your paths straight. Proverbs 3:5-6 NIV

Dad runs a hospital in a small town one hour south of a big city. From the outside, it would make sense that his hospital would stay small. After all, if anyone needed major medical care there are limitless resources less than sixty minutes away. However, my dad is a dreamer. And if he has a dream, he depends on God to show him the path to make that dream come true.

I remember going to a speech he gave once a few years ago and leaving feeling so inspired—which is impressive considering Anthony kept singing "shave it, pluck it, wax it" under his breath after watching a promotional video starring a doctor with the world's largest unibrow. Anyway, unibrow aside, my dad took the example of the Mayo Clinic and compared it to his own hospital. He encouraged his staff that the Mayo story—a premier healthcare facility that started in the middle of nowhere—could be their story too. Then, he laid out a plan.

And guess what? My dad's hospital doubled since he took over 7 years ago, and it's projected to double again in the next four years. I have no doubt it will happen; my dad has faith and isn't afraid to put his faith into action. He makes plans, but submits those plans to God first—never losing sight of his honored house Guest. It doesn't matter if a plan makes sense to the rest of the world, if God wills it to happen it will happen. And yes, I am proud of my dad.

The path of listening to God, and letting Him work through you, is not always easy. One time an old lady who didn't like the way my dad was running the hospital left a death threat on my parent's answering machine. We actually had a pretty good laugh about that one. The message was hilarious. She sounded at least 107 so it was hard to believe she could really break his kneecaps or throw a bomb in his window!

My dad doesn't care what people think...*mostly* in a good way. Some people interpret my dad's intensity as rudeness, but he's not really rude. If he believes God wants him to do something, he does it—even at the expense of his own popularity. He didn't alter his course because one old lady hated, *really hated*, his idea. Ultimately, Dad cares what God thinks and lets that determine the course for his life and the direction of the hospital.

Letting God take control, hosting His presence, being His Friend is not an exhausting job. It's a tremendous relief that will free you to pursue your wildest dreams. Even dreams that seem impossible.

CAPABLE OF AMAZING THINGS

So it's no secret that on my own I can be painfully insecure. But even during my ridiculous "pep talk" days I still had big dreams. I still wanted to do amazing things, but deep down I knew something in me had to change first. I didn't know what it was, but it was something.

The more I identify as a Friend of God, the closer I get to understanding just what it was that was holding me back. And it really wasn't my insecurity. Because, really, on some days I still have a tremendous amount of negative thoughts cross my mind. No, my insecurity is just a temptation. My real problem is where I fix my gaze.

The story of Jesus walking on water (Matthew 14:25-32) in front of a group of His closest personal friends helps me understand my authentic self. Because—yes—Jesus walked on water, but for a time Peter did too. That tells me that Friends of God can walk on water, accomplish the impossible, do amazing things. Verse 25 starts out:

> *Meanwhile, the disciples were in trouble far away from land, for a strong wind had risen, and they were fighting heavy waves. About three o'clock in the morning Jesus came toward them, walking on water.*

You will have trouble. You will fight waves. Being a friend of Jesus doesn't guarantee a cushy life, but it does guarantee a life of Jesus coming toward you. I understand that the world isn't perfect. Once sin entered the world, things just got ugly. I get it. I don't like it, but I can accept things won't be perfect until Jesus comes back. But what I love is that even now, on earth, Jesus comes towards me in miraculous ways:

When the disciples saw him walking on the water, they were terrified. In their fear, they cried out, "It's a ghost!"

But Jesus spoke to them at once. "Don't be afraid," he said. "Take courage. I am here."

You will have trouble, and you will also be afraid. Are you encouraged yet? Gee thanks, trouble *and* fear. But what I like about the Bible is how totally relatable and relevant it is. Everyone is scared sometimes, but as a Friend of God you don't face your fears alone. Friends of God can take courage because He never leaves. Not before the storm, not after the storm, and not smack dab in the middle of the storm:

Then Peter called to him, "Lord if it's really you, tell me to come to you, walking on the water."

"Yes, come," Jesus said.

So Peter went over the side of the boat and walked on the water toward Jesus.

In the past, I would latch on to some part of a verse and use it totally out of context. I took the words of Jesus in one circumstance "do not put the Lord your God to the test" and applied it to everything. I never asked for signs, I never demanded answers. But I wasn't entirely correct in my thinking. Yes, I should respect, and even fear, God. But no, I shouldn't keep my insecurities to myself either. Peter asked Jesus to tell him what to do, and Jesus gave him an answer. **And when Peter fixed his eyes on Jesus, he walked on water too.** Looking to Jesus, and acting on faith, is what makes it possible for friends of Jesus to do the impossible. Finally, look what happens next:

But when he saw the strong wind and the waves, he was terrified and began to sink. "Save me, Lord!" he shouted.

Jesus immediately reached out and grabbed him.

"You have so little faith," Jesus said. "Why did you doubt me?"

When they climbed back into the boat, the wind stopped.

And this is where I'm so much like Peter: *Yes, God! I will attempt the impossible!* I'm bulletproof when my eyes are focused on Jesus, but I sink as soon as I notice the strong wind and the waves around me. Circumstances suddenly loom a little too large and my faith takes a nosedive. Before I know it, I'm floundering.

However, and this is my favorite part, Jesus "immediately reached out and grabbed him." I'm never on my own. Even when my faith is weak, Jesus is still there and will catch me *right away.* If you look at the passage as a whole, "at once" and "immediately" are mentioned three times. Jesus is my Friend and true friends react quickly. And not only does He react quickly, He sticks with me until the wind stops, and even then He still won't leave.

But, again, where I fix my gaze is very important. Psalm 121:1-2 says, "I lift up my eyes to the mountains—where does my help come from? My help comes from the LORD, the Maker of heaven and earth." When life seems too depressing, too overwhelming, too busy all I need to do is look up. Take the hand of my Friend who promises in Isaiah 41:10, "Don't be afraid, for I am with you. Don't be discouraged, for I am your God. I will strengthen you and help you. I will hold you up with my victorious right hand."

As a Friend of God, I can walk on water too. For me, "walking on water" means not caving to my insecure thoughts and tendencies. I can trust the words of Jesus in Mark 9:23b

"Anything is possible if a person believes." Because I know my identity is tied to Jesus who can *always* walk on water that means I can persevere even when life throws unexpected curveballs my way.

Speaking of unexpected curveballs, I'm typing right now at a gorgeous park and a bird (that had a few too many berries) dropped a surprise on my computer. Twice. My surroundings couldn't be prettier right now—the sky is blue, the flowers are in bloom—but that didn't stop the bird from doing what he needed to do. Proof that in this life, crap happens. On top of that, the yard guy just zoomed by on his riding mower and spewed grass clippings all over my stuff and I'm pretty sure a spider just bit my foot.

But at least I can still walk on water, right? Through any storm, large and looming or small and annoying, all I really need to do is look up and grab hold of my Friend's hand.

Authentic ID #3

Bride

Hosea 2:19 promises, "I will make you my wife forever, showing you righteousness and justice, unfailing love and compassion." I can live with that. 2 Corinthians 11:2 also says, "I promised you as a pure Bride to one husband—Christ" and in Ephesians the Church, or body of believers, is described as the Bride. The point is, when you put your faith in Christ, you become a part of the Church, the Bride of Christ.

Revelation, the last book of the Bible, foretells what will happen when Jesus comes back to reclaim His Bride, the Church. As we continue waiting until He returns and makes our union with Him complete—completion that's eternal and unspeakably joyful—we're filled with excitement. Talk about anticipation. I want to run, not walk, down that aisle. After all, it's pretty simple. God is so in love with the Bride and she is so in love with Him that they can't be separated.

Erika—once consumed with others' opinions of her, especially guys'—is learning about her identity as a Bride. This summer, she was a counselor at a camp and the theme of one of the weekly talks was, no kidding, based on the Bride/Groom analogy. Here is what she learned about God's role as the perfect Groom, and her role as the Bride of Christ:

> She (the speaker) talked about how when a Bride gets ready on her wedding day, she doesn't get ready nervous and anxious wondering "oh man, I hope my fiancé is going to be at the end of the alter..." or "Hopefully he doesn't forget me or decide to leave." A Bride gets ready on her wedding day GIDDY and EXCITED with all her friends and family around her because she knows that the love of her life is waiting for her at the end of the aisle.
>
> Similarly for us, Jesus is our Groom waiting patiently for us at the end of the aisle! We can live this life with uncontainable excitement KNOWING that at the end of this life our Groom is waiting expectantly for us so that He can bring us home to live in His house with Him forever. We don't have to live in fear of whether or not Jesus is going to be there waiting for us, we can live this life with our eyes fixed on Him knowing confidently that we are getting ready for an eternity with the love of our life. I loved that analogy.

Ironically enough, it was my husband who first latched on to the concept of believers being Brides before I did. In fact, he spent a good couple of years trying to get me excited about it until he finally changed his strategy. He made me think it was my idea—and then I thought it was great. That man knows me so well.

I used to say I wasn't the kind of girl who dreamed of her wedding day but that's not really true. I had forgotten the stacks upon stacks of drawings I made in second grade of my wedding day. Unfortunately, I was in 2nd grade in the 1980s. Let's all be glad I didn't get married until frizzy perms and huge bangs were a distant memory. Man, I loved (and had) them both.

As for my real wedding day...it was perfect. And even more exciting was our whirlwind romance.

Anthony and I met for the first time on April 26, 2004 and were married before the end of that same year. At the time I lived in Ohio and he lived in Kentucky. Until September it was a long distance romance between two people who hated talking on the phone, but liked writing letters. Social media didn't exist yet—it was heaven! The more I learned about Anthony, the more I liked him. Even my parents thought our relationship was a good idea.

I woke up one day in September, gave my 2 weeks' notice at work and moved to Lexington with no job for a guy who technically wasn't even my boyfriend yet. In fact, on Labor Day at the lake someone said, "Oh, is this your girlfriend?" and Anthony hemmed and hawed, "Umm, I don't know. Ummm, uuuhh. So how about this weather we're having?"

Gee, thanks.

To my surprise, things moved fast after the lake incident. Anthony proposed in October and we were married in December. It was like a fairytale. One of the reasons we were able to get married so fast is because I don't care about details. I just don't. My mom planned the whole thing. I didn't even know what my flowers looked like until I showed up—late, but very happy—the day of the wedding.

However, there was one aspect of the wedding that I did care about A LOT. My dress. I wanted to be a beautiful bride. Even after all this time, I would still pick the same dress if I had it to do again. The dress was strapless with a sweetheart neckline and delicate, barely silver roses swirled on the bottom edge of each of the three flowing layers of Chantilly lace, ending in a train. Loved it. Still do. Plus, it had built-in boobies and was so tight in the waist that even though I gained a few pounds before the wedding you couldn't even tell. If I could wear this dress around in my daily life and not look insane, I would.

Anyway, if you're anything like me, I'm sure you have your own pile of drawings of wedding dresses somewhere. Maybe you even have a secret Pinterest board with every detail of your wedding planned down to the tiniest detail. If that's the case, you will love the Biblical analogy of the perfect Groom (he exists!) and the perfect Bride (it's you!) to describe how God sees you as radiant, gorgeous, and pure...even if you don't feel so pure.

If believers (not a building) are the Church, the Church is the Bride of Christ, and Christ loves us intimately like a Groom would love a Bride that means God sees you as a snow-white Bride and He's the Groom. When I walked down the aisle and Anthony's eyes brimmed with tears, I had never felt so loved. However, Anthony's reaction pales in comparison to how God feels about me. God knows everything—and I mean *everything*— about me yet He loves me still. He waits for me to come to Him, and when I do, His reaction blows Anthony's out of the water.

So, unlike me at twenty, don't waste time worrying about the perfect boyfriend or husband coming along...He already has!

As the Bride of Christ this is how He sees you:

You are altogether beautiful, my darling, beautiful in every way. Song of Solomon 4:7

As a young man marries a young woman, so will your Builder marry you; as a bridegroom rejoices over his bride, so will your God rejoice over you. Isaiah 62:5 NIV

Your love delights me, my treasure, my bride. Your love is better than wine, your perfume more fragrant than spices. Song of Solomon 4:10

Focusing on God's love is fulfilling and won't disappoint. In fact, your whole identity is wrapped up in what He thinks of you. I know if you've been around the block a few times it might be easy to think this concept is for virgins only, but it's not. It's for you. No matter your sexual past, when you put your faith in Christ your sins are washed away. You are a new, flawless creation in Christ. You are a perfect Bride.

Next time you are feeling dirty or used, replace that thought with one of the verses above. Satan may whisper lies that you are damaged, but remember who you really are as a Bride of Christ:

- ☑ **Beautiful.** God sees you as a Bride resplendent in white. Beautiful and pure, no matter your sexual track record.

- ☑ **Worthy.** God saves you not because you are pathetic but because He delights in you. You're worth it to Him.

- ☑ **Why? Because He's Got Your Back.** God supports you and loves you because you are His Bride.

BEAUTIFUL

First of all, let me clear up some lingering weirdness about being a Bride of Christ. I used to hate this analogy because of the sexual connotations, but—mind out of the gutter—it's about intimacy, not sex. When I wrapped my head around that, I felt a lot more comfortable with the comparison. After all, I crave intimacy—knowing and being known.

God made us and knows everything about us. Psalms 139:1 says "O Lord, you have examined my heart and know everything about me." Yet knowing everything, even our ugliest thoughts, He still accepts us because we are His. We are so precious to Him that even the very hairs on our heads are all numbered (Matthew 10:30). God knows you and He loves you madly. Get to know Him. You won't be disappointed.

Proof He wants to know us in an *intimate* way:

And Solomon, my son, learn to know the God of your ancestors intimately. Worship and serve him with your whole heart and a willing mind. For the LORD sees every heart and knows every plan and thought. 1 Chronicles 28:9a

But just in case you're wondering: *Eek—can I really still wear a white dress?*

The answer is yes. Yes, you can. The word "purity" drives me nuts because people tend to use is as a weapon—or at the very least, as a tool to make people feel bad. But guess what? No matter how many people you've slept with, no matter how you've been used or abused you are made pure—totally pure—when you put your faith in Christ.

I knew one couple who bragged about not having sex before marriage. Well, it turns out they had other skeletons in their closets because their relationship didn't last long. I've heard of others who engage in all sorts of crazy sexual antics—and as long as they don't technically have actual sex—they sort of lord it over people.

Sheesh. It's about your heart. If you don't feel pure, you can. It will take some discipline on your part, but read what God says about purity. Don't listen to what others say, listen to what He says. Yes, your actions matter. They absolutely, positively do. We are told to be sexually pure (and even this comes from a place of love—sex within marriage is consequence free, but can this be said about sex outside marriage?). However, your past actions are forgiven. Once you place your faith in Christ, you are white dress qualified.

Once you grasp that you are clean because your *heart* is clean, your actions will follow suit. You have self-control. You have discipline. But focusing on the action of self-control without realizing why you have it does no good. It's the whole feel dirty/live dirty concept all over again. So go ahead and accept that you *can* wear white:

> For husbands, this means love your wives, just as Christ loved the church. He gave up his life for her to make her holy and clean, washed by the cleansing of God's word. He did this to present her to himself as a glorious church without a spot or wrinkle or any other blemish. Instead, she will be holy and without fault. Ephesians 5:27

Again, through faith in Christ *you are without a spot or wrinkle or any other blemish.* Your dress is white because He made it that way through His sacrifice; it is finished, through faith you are clean. You don't have to stoop over a sink forever scrubbing stains. You need to believe if God says you are worthy, through faith you are worthy.

And don't underestimate how *beautiful* you are to your Groom. In fact, this is what He is thinking when you walk down the aisle:

How beautiful you are and how pleasing, my love, with your delights! Song of Solomon 7:6

> *You have stolen my heart, my sister, my Bride; you have stolen my heart with one glance of your eyes, with one jewel of your necklace. Song of Solomon 4:9*

WORTHY

I love the *30 for 30* ESPN documentaries about athletes (not the actual sports) on Netflix. We watched one the other day called *Broke* that stayed with me for days. According to the show 78% of professional athletes are flat broke in two years. Flat broke in two years?! I couldn't believe it. The ironic part is while they are playing and earning millions upon millions, women flock to clubs just to snag one of them...even for a night. There is even a website that announces "baller alerts" so women anxious to hook up with a professional athlete know where to go!

One former athlete on the show, now broke and living in squalor, fathered 9 kids by 9 women. From the outside he may have originally looked like Prince Charming. He had the potential to "save" women with his millions, right? But in the end, he was broke and hurting—desperate to relive the glory days, bitter and brooding. His eyes were so sad.

If a rich, strong, handsome professional athlete is no real knight on a white horse in the end—what's a girl to do? I won't get into the infidelity, accusations, abnormally high divorce rates, and other depressing tidbits to prove a human (no matter how spectacular) can't save you. However, like Erika shared earlier, you don't have to settle for a mere knight when you can have a King.

My favorite verse really drives home the idea of a real Prince Charming:

The Lord your God is with you; the Mighty Warrior who saves. In his love, he no longer rebukes you but rejoices over you with singing. Zephaniah 3:17 NIV

You have a champion. God is your real knight on a white horse, and He is the only One who has the ability to save. No one can save herself (or himself for that matter). When I tried to save myself, I only felt more and more hopeless. I was embarrassed and defensive about the state of my life. I was in a mess, but would have rather died than admit that I felt like a damsel in distress.

What shocked me was that even when my life was in total disarray God didn't see me as a pathetic, weak damsel in distress. He saw me as a beautiful, capable woman who had the potential to do great things for His name's sake, but was simply struggling to see any good or potential in herself. My faith, even at its weakest, mattered more than my behavior (which was influenced so heavily by my feelings of inadequacy).

God sees the same strong, capable woman in you too. That's why the Mighty Warrior saves you: You are worth saving. You are not helpless or hopeless...unless you allow yourself to be. God can save you and the bravest thing you can do is put your faith in Him. Admit you can't do it on your own.

For me, admitting I needed to be rescued was my biggest act of strength. Everyone, no matter how strong, needs a champion. In fact, we should feel empowered because 2 Timothy 1:7 says, "For God has not given us a spirit of fear and timidity, but of power, love and a sound mind." We have a powerful spirit, that's for sure, but that doesn't mean life won't be hard. That's why a Mighty Warrior is necessary.

No matter your circumstances, He can save you. After He saves you, He won't abandon you either. When He delights in you, it's not for one night or based on your level of enthusiasm.

Nor does He save you only to make you feel bad about yourself later. He really, truly rejoices over you.

In the original language, the phrase "rejoices over you" is really a picture of God dancing with you, twirling until you both get swept up in the sky. Zephaniah 3:17 is the ultimate first dance, with a Groom who never disappoints. You are so deeply, deeply loved. You have a protector, a guide, a perfect husband. He respects His Bride and finds her delightful. Realizing God delights in me changed my life, and I hope it changes yours.

While for whatever twisted reason I enjoy depressing ESPN mini-documentaries, I also love Disney movies. I'm so glad I have kids so I can pretend our massive collection is for them. Rapunzel has Eugene, Anna has Kristoff. That's all I ever wanted. To be so loved a man would risk his life for me. To see good in me when I couldn't quite see any myself.

Well, done and done. I am that loved. Christ died for me. He delights in me and cannot wait to see me walk down the aisle and enter a relationship with Him. Also, and I mean this from the bottom of my heart, my relationship with God gets more and more and more exciting as it grows deeper. Marriages may fail, but God's role as my perfect Groom will never leave me shortchanged.

Once I accepted that Zephaniah 3:17 was true—and my real Prince Charming would stick around after He saved me—I started really enjoying His presence in my life. I couldn't say that until somewhat recently. I wasted years following God out of fear, duty, and guilt. And I felt defeated most of the time. No matter how many times I swore I would change, the pressure eventually made me explode.

From my experience, a guilt/duty/fear-only based relationship with God is no way to live. It's setting yourself up for failure because you *will* mess up. You will fall down. And if your safety net is warped and gaping with holes, you won't bounce back.

I adapted these 2 examples from John Piper to explain how our motivation for following God affects our relationship:

1. Say your fiancé buys you flowers and slams them on the table saying, "Here you go. Bought these because I know I have to and I don't want to hear you complain later that I never get you anything." After he flops on the couch to watch TV, I seriously doubt you feel appreciated and loved. He only bought the flowers because he had to, not because he wanted to.

2. Now, if your fiancé gave you flowers and says "I bought these for you because I love you so much. You do so many good things for me no matter what kind of mood I'm in, and I know this is not much, but I wanted to give you something to show how much I care. I just can't wait to marry you." I'm pretty sure you would be thrilled. He bought the flowers because he loves and appreciates you; he wanted to buy them to show you how much.

My relationship with God used to be based on duty just like example #1. I served God because I felt like I should, like I had to. Truthfully, I didn't want to, I wanted to do whatever I wanted without consequence and then get all the benefits of a relationship with God too: peace, patience, contentment. And I didn't really think God was interested in me either.

However, my own sin shot up a barrier between God and me. To overcome this barrier that blocked communication with God, I would slam some figurative flowers on His coffee table and say, "are we even, now? Can I have my peace back?" I would feel rotten about stuff I did, swear I would never do a certain bad thing again, do some good things to make up for it, fall back down again, and repeat the cycle. Trying to please God based on guilt was exhausting.

Example #2 shows how a love based relationship with God is a *much* better way to live. When we love God because He first loves us, we won't burn out. Picture yourself as a teacup. God pours His love from His teapot into your cup until it overflows. If you operate out of appreciation for what God has done for you, and constantly allow His love to pour into you, then when you love others you are only giving away the overflow of extra love. It is rejuvenating. And it's okay if your teacup has a few cracks. That allows more love to flow through you.

It's not to say we shouldn't fear God. Just ask the crazies holding the "YOU ARE GOING TO HELL" posters or yelling "YOU ARE A SLUT!!!" to every girl in a pair of shorts an inch above her knee on college campuses across the nation. Sorry, "crazies" wasn't very nice but I think they are only telling half the story. Yes, God is all-powerful. He could wipe us out in a second if He so inclined, but He doesn't. He made us, loves us, and desires a relationship with us.

Sin does need to be paid for. And I think by now we can all admit that when we live in complete and utter selfishness we are *eventually* miserable. In the midst of sin, it sure is fun but it gets old sooner or later. Sin sucks. It's agony. Always has been, always will be. So—yes—we absolutely need to acknowledge before God that we are indeed flawed people who sin and make mistakes.

We need the sacrifice of Jesus to erase our sins so we can be made right with God through Him. On our own, we will never measure up. However, once again, we are not alone. God loved us so unbelievably much He sent His son to pay the price of our sins for us.

See the balance? **You have to accept the power of God *and* the love of God.** Ephesians 3:19 says, "May you experience the love of Christ, though it is too great to understand fully. Then you will be made complete with all the fullness of life and power that comes from God." God loves you so much. You don't suck.

Now my desire to follow God is based on love. I'm eager to know Him because I know He is eager to know me. Erika's motivation for trusting God in based on love now too. In fact, the reason Erika enjoyed the speaker at her camp so much is because of how following God out of love relates to the Bride/Groom analogy. She loves Him because He loves her, not because she's afraid or feels guilty:

> *...She (the speaker) used Revelation 19:7-8 which says "The wedding day of the Lamb has come and his Bride has made herself ready. She was allowed to wear a bright, clean linen garment." I love the end of that because every little girl dreams of wearing a white wedding dress...and because of Jesus' sacrifice, we are wiped clean, made new, and able to come before our Father wearing a beautiful and pure white garment...*

> *We also talked about verse 11 in chapter 19 of Revelations how it says "there was a white horse and its rider was called Faithful and True" which shows that not only is Jesus our Groom, even better He's our PRINCE CHARMING! He doesn't just come grab our hand and drag us into Heaven, He comes for us on a white horse—just like out of a fairytale! He is called Faithful and True, two things I know I for sure want to see in my husband!*

Jesus comes back on a white horse and His name is "Faithful and True." And like Erika said, these two qualities—not riches or fame—are what I really want in a man. Revelations goes on to say our Prince Charming is fair and just, wears many crowns, and His robe symbolizes His crucifixion. He leads a heavenly army to come rescue His Bride and strike down our enemies to demonstrate His authority as King of all kings.

Now we're talking. My identity as a Bride of Christ proves I have a champion who will never ever leave. He will right all wrongs and fight for me. He sees me as a Bride on her wedding day and invites me to share in His riches. And unlike a pro athlete, His riches last.

WHY? HE'S GOT YOUR BACK

Dear Mommy,

Here is a song that I wrote just for you!

You are the master of my side,

The one and only master of my ride!

I have your back.

Rylie

My little girl wrote this song the summer after kindergarten (she's so smart!) on mint green and pink construction paper cut into the shape of a long, skinny heart. My prized possession. Rylie can criticize the way I fry bacon, but you better not. She has my back. And I have hers.

I think marriage is appealing because ideally it means someone always has your back. And people will take issue with you. It happened to me a couple months ago.

It all started when I made a mistake. A friend and I had an awkward disagreement and I handled the situation wrong. Then, when I talked to her about it later, she hurt my feelings. I knew she would be mad, but I didn't expect her words to be so harsh. She had some strong opinions, and her tone made me want to crawl in a hole. The part that bothered me is I just hate conflict. I want everyone to like me. Everyone. If someone doesn't like me, I can't help but think up A.) a hundred ways to get her to like me; or B.) a million ways to trash talk her to someone else to make myself feel better. It makes me feel weak and like giving up.

However, I can cower under harsh words and not being liked (which when it boils down to it is just plain selfish), or I can stand strong. As a child of God, I am powerful because of Christ's death and resurrection. He has my back. Romans 8:11 says, "The Spirit of God, who raised Jesus from the dead, lives in you. And just as God raised Christ Jesus from the dead, he will give life to your mortal bodies by this same Spirit living within you."

When I mess up, I can ask forgiveness and if the person doesn't accept it, I can move on. I'm not perfect, and that's okay. I don't have to be timid and scared about my imperfections or hide under a rock to avoid conflict (although that sounds appealing) because the same power that raised Christ from the dead lives in me.

There have been times when Anthony has had my back, and times when he didn't. Even the most dependable, trustworthy people are still people. Flawed at best. But Christ, our perfect Groom, is just that: perfect and dependable.

In 2 Corinthians 12:9 Paul says, "But he said to me, 'My grace is sufficient for you, for my power is made perfect in weakness.' Therefore I will boast all the more gladly of my weaknesses, so that the power of Christ may rest upon me." If you feel weak like I do sometimes, think of it as an opportunity for Christ's power to take over. As a Bride of God, you don't have to give up when a weakness flares up in your life. When your strength gives out, His kicks in. He is the partner who never quits, never leaves your side. He is the master of your ride:

> In him we have redemption through his blood, the forgiveness of sins, in accordance with the riches of God's grace that he lavished on us. With all wisdom and understanding, I pray that the eyes of your heart may be

enlightened in order that you may know the hope to which he has called you, the riches of his glorious inheritance in his holy people, and his incomparably great power for us who believe. That power is the same as the mighty strength he exerted when he raised Christ from the dead and seated him at his right hand in the heavenly realms. Ephesians 1:7, 8, 18-20 NIV

P.S. When she was three, I overheard Rylie teaching her brother one of her songs on their little toy piano. The title? *Killer Whales Attacking Christmas.* Her gift is clearly creativity. Having her back is so much fun.

Bask in the joy of being a beautiful Bride. Get excited. Giddy. It's okay to enjoy your Groom; He enjoys you. Heck, write a song about it.

PART 4

The Choice

The Choice

Are you going to rely on yourself or God? At the end of the day, that's the real choice. The only choice. Other stuff matters, very much actually, but when you boil it all down that's what is left.

I'm either way too hard or not hard enough on myself. I'm a heap of contradictions and insecurities, but that's not all I am. Knowing God sees me as worthwhile heals my warped perceptions and gives me deep-rooted security. When I hear "be yourself" it actually comforts me instead of giving me a heart attack. I'm no longer as confused.

I am God's Daughter, God's Friend, and God's Bride. I'm wanted, loved, accepted, forgiven, redeemed. It feels good, a huge relief. It's the big stuff. And when I figured out the big stuff and chose to believe it, all the little stuff—like my talents and interests—began to unfold as well.

It's important to know that God desires all of you, and I know that's hard. You can be The Life of the Party Saturday night and The Perfect Christian Sunday morning. But that gets old fast, the old double-life routine. I've been there and giving up the

Saturday/Sunday versions of myself was one of the most freeing things I've ever done.

The importance of the choice is the desire of your heart and not necessarily your actions. If the desire is there, the actions will soon follow. Sometimes we flip back and forth quickly, but in the end if you don't give your whole self to God with an uppercase G, that part of you that is compromising will become your god too. Little gods destroy us, big God builds us up.

When I was desperate enough to truly give God a shot, I was shocked that my New Creation self was still capable of some very Fake ID behavior. But I am learning that guilt is connected to our actions, not our identities. Shame is a lie that tells us our bad actions are who we are. Or in other words, guilt says, "I did something bad" and shame says, "I am bad." There is a difference.

The Bible tells me that as a New Creation I am a saint. Even if I screw up and steal a tube of lipstick I am still a saint. However, shame tricks me into thinking, "I stole so now I'm a thief." Yes, stealing is wrong but it's not an identity. It's a verb. An action. And actions can change.

And change takes time. Don't be too hard on yourself. You are getting to know a whole new version of yourself and it will take time to adjust. I promise that no matter how excited you are about following God, you will make more mistakes. Don't let guilty feelings keep you down.

Keep in mind that repentance does not mean "feel like crap," it means "change." If you do something wrong, the Holy Spirit will convict you to change (possibly through guilt) not condemn you (make you feel ashamed) for a past mistake for which you've already received forgiveness.

Besides, allowing shame to control you is basically the same as telling God that the sacrifice of Jesus was just not enough. Your sins were too big. His death too small. And that's just insulting. God is never small. You don't have to heap more punishment on yourself because His crucifixion was plenty punishment enough.

Guilt can lead to repentance, but if there's nothing to repent of, it's shame—not guilt. God convicts and lifts you to a better place, but Satan condemns and forces you farther down the pit of despair. If you trust Jesus and ask God to forgive you, you are forgiven on His merit. We're responsible to change too, but God helps us with that part as we walk with Him. God's part is forgiving us; our part is to accept the forgiveness through Christ.*

A good example of repentance is found in Matthew 26 & 27 when two of Jesus' closest friends betrayed Him on the same night. Judas and Peter flattered Jesus to His face during a feast and swore they would never forsake Him when He predicted their betrayal and denial. In verse 25 Judas says, "Surely you don't mean me, Rabbi?" in regards to his imminent betrayal and in verse 33 Peter says, "Even if all fall away on account of you, I never will."

Despite the protests of Judas and Peter, later that night they both turned their backs on Jesus. Some jealous religious leaders wanted Jesus dead, and Judas agreed to hand Jesus over to them for 30 pieces of silver. The same price as a slave. Once in the hands of the religious leaders, Peter denied knowing Jesus

*FOOTNOTE *When I mention "through Jesus" or "trust/faith in Jesus" what I mean is relying on or trusting in Jesus and making him king/boss of your life is what makes you a believer, a "Christian." Check out www.laneofroses.com for more information.*

three times outside the very gates where Jesus was being tried, persecuted, and condemned to die on the cross.

Both men failed Jesus, but their reactions to their sins are significant. Peter repented, meaning he asked forgiveness, trusted he was forgiven, and changed. He went on to be the leader of the first church. However, Judas just felt shameful and used his 30 coins to purchase the land on which he committed suicide. See the difference? Both sinned, granted in very different ways, but their reactions led to totally opposite outcomes.

Feeling guilty and bad won't make you closer to God. In fact, shame can make you more susceptible to believing lies. Repenting will bring you near to God. And remember, He always tells the truth. **You are loved for being His, not for being perfect.**

In fact, Jesus tells us in Matthew 22:34-40:

But when the Pharisees heard that he had silenced the Sadducees with his reply, they met together to question him again. One of them, an expert in religious law, tried to trap him with this question: "Teacher, which is the most important commandment in the law of Moses?"

Jesus replied, "'You must love the LORD your God with all your heart, all your soul, and all your mind.' This is the first and greatest commandment. A second is equally important: 'Love your neighbor as yourself.' The entire law and all the demands of the prophets are based on these two commandments."

Get it? Love, not rules, is what is most important. If you base your identity on how well you follow rules, you will end up creating another Fake ID. It might not be "The Girlfriend" anymore, but "The Perfect Christian" can be just as empty.

When I first switched from relying on myself to relying on God, it was frustrating. I didn't magically love Bible-reading and found some of my other fellow Perfect Christians (very) tedious.

But I was a little confused about the rules of following God.

To my surprise, the only "rules" to follow as Christian are 1.) Love God; and 2.) Love Others. That's it. All other rules fall under the umbrella of love. If you truly love others, you probably won't kill anyone anyway.

In the New Testament, the Jewish religious leaders had the Ten Commandments down pat. They were excellent rule followers, but had unforgiving hearts. On the Sermon on the Mount in Matthew 5-7 Jesus warns the crowd of religious zealots and everyday citizens that following rules doesn't make you right with God. In fact, Jesus adds to the rules to show how they are impossible to follow through.

For example in Matthew 5:27 Jesus says, "You have heard the commandment that says, 'You must not commit adultery.' But I say, anyone who even looks at a woman with lust has already committed adultery with her in his heart." Okay. Enough said. My husband works with some awesome fraternity guys. They are sweet, but—man—they like the ladies. If they had to get to heaven based on following this rule, I'm not sure they'd make it. Sorry guys.

However, if you read what comes right before the extra layers of perfection and rules that Jesus lays out, you will notice that rules aren't the point. He used hyperbole to show the hoity-toity religious leaders that following rules perfectly is impossible. If you count on flawless behavior as your ticket to Heaven, you won't make it. In Matthew 5:17 Jesus explains, "Don't misunderstand why I have come. I did not come to abolish the law of Moses or the writings of the prophets. No I came to accomplish their purpose."

So, if you are pressuring yourself to follow rules to restore your relationship with God, you are barking up the wrong tree. Relieve yourself of the pressure to be perfect. Breathe a deep sigh of relief—*ahhhh*—and know that Jesus fulfilled the requirements of the Old Testament for you. His perfection fills in the gaps of all of your mistakes. You don't have to be a slave to rules anymore. However, as your heart fills with love, your actions will change. It might not happen overnight, but it will happen. Don't give up:

> *Never tire of doing right for at the proper time you will reap a harvest if you don't give up. Galatians 6:9 NIV*

No matter what you've done, if you relate to the prodigal or his brother or both, remember that you're invited to the party. God wants you. I want you there too. I want you there too not because following God is a special club full of know-it-alls, but because life with God is peace, hope, and—best of all—rest. My burdens are lifted, and that more than anything is what keeps me going.

The choice to accept or decline is up to you. You're loved either way, but saying yes to that love is what will change your life. It certainly changed mine.

I think that's why every time I say "You don't suck," girls cry. That's why I wrote this book. After all, isn't that what we all want to hear? We are loveable. We don't suck. I know I cried when I first found out. Honestly, I still cry about it sometimes. That's why I can't shut up about it.

The reason why we don't suck is that our identities are not bound by our past decisions. So you were a dork in high school, does that mean you're forever a dork? You slept around with any and every one, does that make you a slut now? Of course not. In fact, even in your dorkiest, darkest moments you weren't a dork or a slut. You can let that go.

You were fearfully and wonderfully made. Read Psalm 139. Read Psalm 103. You are forgiven, a New Creation created in advance to do good things that God planned especially for you. Don't let feelings of inadequacy or lies prevent you from living out your full potential.

One of the writers of the New Testament, Matthew, was a despicable guy before he met Jesus. He was by all accounts "scum." The snobbish religious leaders in his town called him names and thought he was beneath them. However, Jesus didn't see Matthew as scum, Jesus saw him based on his potential.

God sees you based on your potential too. It may not feel like it now, but your broken heart is fixable. Choose to believe what God thinks about you. Choose to accept your Authentic Identity.

After all, you don't suck.

— Fake IDs —

HELPFUL CHART FOR HORRIBLE DAYS

Memorize the following chart as a way to prepare yourself when lies threaten to consume you. You are a New Creation. God's Daughter, Friend, and Bride. He loves you so much.

> *Don't copy the behavior and customs of this world, but let God transform you into a new person by changing the way you think. Romans 12:2a*

Replace Fake ID thoughts... *My worth is tied to my relationship status, performance, or popularity.*	**... with Authentic ID thoughts!** *This means that anyone who belongs to Christ has become a new person. The old life is gone; a new life has begun!* 2 Corinthians 5:17
I'm unforgivable.	**I am forgiven.** *He has removed our sins as far from us as the east is from the west.* Psalm 103:12
I'm weak.	**I am courageous.** *For God has not given us a spirit of fear and timidity, but of power, love and a sound mind.* 2 Timothy 1:7
I'm a lost cause.	**I am redeemed.** *Instead of shame and dishonor, you will enjoy a double share of honor.* Isaiah 61:7a
I'm unacceptable.	**I am accepted.** *Therefore, accept each other just as Christ has accepted you so that God will be given glory.* Romans 15:7
I'm unlovable.	**I'm loved.** *For the L*ord *your God is living among you.* He is a mighty savior. He will take delight in you with gladness. With his love, he will calm all your fears. He will rejoice over you with joyful songs. *Zephaniah 3:17*

I can't.	**Through Christ, I can.** *For I can do everything through Christ, who gives me strength.* Philippians 4:13
I'm dirty.	**I'm clean.** *And I will give you a new heart, and I will put a new spirit in you. I will take out your stony, stubborn heart and give you a tender, responsive heart.* Ezekiel 36:26
I'm worthless.	**I'm worthy.** *For we are God's masterpiece. He has created us anew in Christ Jesus, so we can do the good things he planned for us long ago.* Ephesians 2:10
I'm alone.	**I am never alone.** *Do not be afraid or discouraged, for the Lord will personally go ahead of you. He will be with you; he will neither fail you nor abandon you.* Deuteronomy 31:8

Helpful Chart for Horrible Days

(Tear this one out and put it somewhere you will see it everyday!)
For more free resources and tips see www.laneofroses.com.

Memorize the following chart as a way to prepare yourself when lies threaten to consume you. You are a New Creation. God's Daughter, Friend, and Bride. He loves you so much.

Don't copy the behavior and customs of this world, but let God transform you into a new person by changing the way you think. Romans 12:2a

Replace Fake ID thoughts... *My worth is tied to my relationship status, performance, or popularity.*	... with Authentic ID thoughts! *This means that anyone who belongs to Christ has become a new person. The old life is gone; a new life has begun!* 2 Corinthians 5:17
I'm unforgivable.	I am forgiven. *He has removed our sins as far from us as the east is from the west.* Psalm 103:12
I'm weak.	I am courageous. *For God has not given us a spirit of fear and timidity, but of power, love and a sound mind.* 2 Timothy 1:7
I'm a lost cause.	I am redeemed. *Instead of shame and dishonor, you will enjoy a double share of honor.* Isaiah 61:7a
I'm unacceptable.	I am accepted. *Therefore, accept each other just as Christ has accepted you so that God will be given glory.* Romans 15:7
I'm unlovable.	I'm loved. *For the LORD your God is living among you. He is a mighty savior. He will take delight in you with gladness. With his love, he will calm all your fears. He will rejoice over you with joyful songs.* Zephaniah 3:17

I can't.	**Through Christ, I can.** *For I can do everything through Christ, who gives me strength.* Philippians 4:13
I'm dirty.	**I'm clean.** *And I will give you a new heart, and I will put a new spirit in you. I will take out your stony, stubborn heart and give you a tender, responsive heart.* Ezekiel 36:26
I'm worthless.	**I'm worthy.** *For we are God's masterpiece. He has created us anew in Christ Jesus, so we can do the good things he planned for us long ago.* Ephesians 2:10
I'm alone.	**I am never alone.** *Do not be afraid or discouraged, for the Lord will personally go ahead of you. He will be with you; he will neither fail you nor abandon you.* Deuteronomy 31:8

Author's Note

Dear Reader,

Eleven years ago I was at my lowest. It was at this low point that I thought "I just can't do this anymore." I was tired of believing lies, and this realization was the slap in the face that finally woke me up and made me think, "God surely has more for me than this."

I've not been the same since—and not because I believed more in myself or suddenly had a surge in self-esteem. Far from it! I stopped relying on myself and got to know the true character of God. The more I understood how much He radically loves me, the more I trusted Him, and the more my behavior changed as a result of experiencing such security and hope.

And now? I'm learning that it's okay to feel good about myself. I am confident because my confidence is in God. He never changes, never stops loving me. Today, I am still far from perfect—and my circumstances aren't always perfect either—but I have hope. And my hope is strong. My hope is secure.

So what do I hope you take away from *Fake IDs*? That God loves you. That He really, really loves you. Despite your past, despite your present, you are valuable in the eyes of God. I've already prayed for everyone who reads this book. Why? Because I know how hard it is to accept God's acceptance.

Finally, please be sure to check out www.laneofroses.com. On the website you will find information on how to start a relationship with God and the counseling services I mention several times throughout the book. Also, you can do a keyword search for the full stories of Melody, Erika, and Grace Ann. And who knows? Maybe it's even time for you to share your story and encourage someone else who might relate to your own faith journey:

Counseling Services:
http://www.laneofroses.org/#!counseling-services/c12bz
Start a Relationship with God:

http://www.laneofroses.org/#!start-a-relationship-with-god/c101z

Places to Connect: http://www.laneofroses.org/#!places-to-connect/cca5

Love & best wishes,

Katie

katie@laneofroses.com

CPSIA information can be obtained at www.ICGtesting.com
Printed in the USA
LVOW11s0315270815

451698LV00001B/2/P